SHAMBHALA DRAGON EDITIONS

The dragon is an age-old symbol of the highest spiritual essence, embodying wisdom, strength, and the divine power of transformation. In this spirit, Shambhala Dragon Editions offers a treasury of readings in the sacred knowledge of Asia. In presenting the works of authors both ancient and modern, we seek to make these teachings accessible to lovers of wisdom everywhere.

Each Shambhala Dragon Edition features Smyth-sewn binding and is printed on acid-free paper.

WORLDLY WISDOM

Confucian Teachings
of the Ming Dynasty

Translated and edited by
J. C. CLEARY

SHAMBHALA
Boston & London
1991

AMBHALA PUBLICATIONS, INC.
orticultural Hall
0 Massachusetts Avenue
ston, Massachusetts 02115
vw.shambhala.com

inted in the United States of America

stributed in the United States by Random House, Inc.,
d in Canada by Random House of Canada Ltd

BRARY OF CONGRESS CATALOGING-IN-PUBLICATION DATA

orldly wisdom : Confucian teachings of the Ming Dynasty / translated and edited
by J. C. Cleary—1st Shambhala ed.
p. cm.—(Shambhala dragon editions)
ISBN 1-57062-701-0
1. Confucianism. 2. Philosophy, Confucian. I. Cleary, J.C. (Jonathan Christopher)
BL1830.W67 1991 90-42220
181′.112–dc20 CIP

BVG 01

To my wife

Thương mến tặng Mai, với lòng biết ơn sâu xa

CONTENTS

·

INTRODUCTION:
    THE CONFUCIAN TRADITION   ix

WU YUBI   1
HU JUREN   4
XUE XUAN   8
XIA SHANGPU   15
LÜ NAN   18
ZHAN RUOSHUI   25
HONG YUAN   29
FENG CONGWU   31
WANG YANGMING   35
WANG JI   46
QIAN DEHONG   54
WANG GEN   60
ZOU SHOUYI   64
OUYANG DE   73
NIE BAO   75
LUO HONGXIAN   81
LIU WENMIN   91
CHEN JIUCHUAN   94
WAN TINGYAN   97
ZHOU CHONG   100
ZHU DEZHI   101
XUE YINGQI   103
ZHA SHENGDUO   104
TANG SHUNZHI   107
XU JIE   112
YANG YUSUN   116
LUO RUFANG   117

Contents

GENG DINGXIANG	121
XU YONGJIAN	125
ZHANG YUANBIAN	130
WANG SHIHUAI	135
ZOU YUANBIAO	145
JIAO HONG	153
ZHU SHILU	156
LUO QINSHUN	159
LI ZHONG	162
LÜ KUN	165

INTRODUCTION

The Confucian Tradition

.

Like China itself, the Confucian tradition has had a long and intricate history of evolution and development. From the time of Confucius twenty-five hundred years ago up until the present day, the Confucian teaching has appeared in many forms. During the Middle Ages, Confucianism spread out from China to Korea, to Vietnam, and to Japan. For many centuries it has played a major role in East Asian civilization in the realms of politics and philosophy, ethics and social practice, ideas and beliefs.

As we try to answer the call of modern times to break out of our limited parochial views of the human condition, we cannot afford to overlook a tradition that has been alive for so long among such a large part of humankind.

For Westerners, there are various factors that have made it hard to come to grips with Confucianism. The style of many Confucian writings reflects a culture that is quite foreign to us. It is easy to be distracted by the exotic surface and fail to appreciate the underlying commonality of human concerns. Moreover, Confucian thought cuts across the categories that our own culture has taught us to accept as normal and natural. Confucianism shares the traits of both religion and philosophy, so it is futile to insist on one or the other of these Western labels. Confucian thinkers treated as an integral whole what we divide into personal ethics on the one hand and social thought and politics on the other. In the Confucian tradition, inner-directed contemplative pursuits and outwardly involved social action are viewed not as alternatives but as equally necessary, complementary aspects of the work of human self-cultivation.

These differences of style and substance have made it hard for Westerners to appreciate the Confucian tradition for what it is. There has been a natural tendency in Western accounts of Confucianism to seize on certain themes, overemphasize them, and thus give an unbalanced picture of the tradition as a whole.

ix

Introduction

With East Asia assuming greater prominence on the world scene, it is time for us to see beyond the standard clichés and misconceptions and get a deeper, more accurate view of Confucianism. I think the best way to do this is to look directly at authentic Confucian sources.

This book presents a selection of passages from leading Confucian thinkers of the early modern period, the Chinese contemporaries of Erasmus and Luther, Machiavelli and Galileo. This was a protean period in the history of China, as in the history of our own culture, when age-old notions were reconsidered and many new ideas emerged. By this time too, Confucianism had been greatly enriched by its interactions with Buddhism and Taoism. Readers who bring with them the usual images of Confucianism should be ready for a surprise.

Over its long history, the Confucian tradition has been elaborated by many outstanding thinkers who have produced various formulations of its key ideas, with shifting patterns of emphasis. Nevertheless, it is possible to pick out a consistent core of basic concerns that are fundamental to the Confucian worldview. In order to appreciate the primary sources translated in this work, the reader should be familiar with this core of fundamental Confucian ideas.

First and foremost, Confucianism is a humanistic teaching. It focuses on human life in this world, not on preparing for a life to come, and emphasizes people's relationships with each other, not their dealings with the supernatural. It is concerned with how people should develop their personalities, how to conduct social relations, and how best to order human society.

In Confucian eyes, all these questions are intimately related: humans are preeminently social beings, and human life takes place within a network of social relations. The full realization of human potential depends on the proper cultivation of relationships with other people and on properly fulfilling one's role within society as a whole.

Confucianism is profoundly humanistic, but it would be wrong to overlook the religious dimensions in both its theory and its practice. The proper norms of human life are the main focus, but these are understood as being derived from the cosmic order, from the Tao of Heaven. In daily life, one of the primary values of Confucianism is reverence, an attitude of respect for life and serious attention to moral duty, that is, a scrupulous concern to follow the patterns of the Tao in all areas.

In the past, some Westerners have been so befuddled by the notion that Christianity is the model for what all religions must be like that they have denied that Confucianism is a religion at all. They have claimed that Confucianism is "only" a philosophy, a system of ethics, a way of life.

But the Confucian tradition includes all the key elements that are commonly thought to make up religion: it has a comprehensive system of beliefs that explain mankind's place in the universe and provide norms for human conduct, it has exemplary teachers, it has scriptures, it even has temples and rituals. Like other religions, Confucianism was a major political force. And of course Confucianism played a central guiding role in the lives of its believers, just as the other religious faiths did with theirs.

In the Confucian worldview, Heaven plays a role that is analogous to the role of God in the "Western" (actually Middle Eastern) theistic religions. The degree to which Heaven is personified in the Confucian classics varies, but overall an impersonal image prevails. Though Heaven is normally not personified to the degree that God is in Judaism, Christianity, and Islam, it would be an ethnocentric mistake to speak of Confucianism as atheistic. Like God, Heaven has given us life, endowed us with our human nature, and given us rules to live by. In the Confucian worldview, Heaven stands above the human world and provides the basic pattern for the proper ordering of human affairs. If human conduct departs from the true pattern mandated by Heaven, this invites disaster. Confucius said, "He who offends against Heaven has nowhere to turn to pray for relief" (*Lunyu*, 3.13).

To Confucians, the human order is part of the cosmic order and must obey its principles. The concept of the Tao refers both to the cosmic order and to the normative order for human affairs: the Tao is manifest in natural law and also in moral law. Heaven's true pattern is inherent in the human mind, as in all things, and provides us with the blueprint for human relations and social order. Ethical principles and the constant norms of human behavior are part of this true pattern. Heaven has endowed us with our true nature, and Heaven has decreed that to be truly human we must follow this true nature.

Confucianism is preeminently a moral teaching. It focuses on moral norms and proper standards for conduct. In Confucian eyes, humans are moral beings: moral standards are an inherent part of human nature, which is basically good. The necessary elements for morality are present in embryo in the true nature that Heaven has endowed us with, and can be developed by education.

The moral standpoint of the Confucian tradition is best revealed in its classic values.

First is *ren,* human fellow-feeling (sometimes translated as "true humanity," "humaneness," or "benevolence"). This refers to the basic solidarity that allows people to empathize with each other and gives them the innate impulse to do the decent thing. "What you do not want done to you, do not do to others" is the Confucian version of our Golden Rule. The requirements of *ren,* of true humanity, are discussed in detail by Confucius in the *Analects.*

Another cardinal virtue is *yi,* the sense of moral duty (sometimes translated as "righteousness"). According to the Confucian teaching, there are absolute standards of righteousness, of moral obligation, that must govern all social relations. A classic Confucian maxim declares, "To see what your duty is and not do it is cowardice." At the social-political level, the Confucian classic called *The Great Learning* teaches that "what is advantageous to a nation is not profit, but righteousness."

The Confucian tradition also places great emphasis on *li,* the proper norms of conduct (also translated literally as "rites" and "etiquette"). A good society is possible only when the members of society hold to the moral rules proper to their social roles. Confucius himself was very critical of what he saw as the breakdown of the proper norms of conduct in the society in which he lived. A common Confucian admonition speaks of "controlling oneself and returning to the proper norms." The proper norms include solidarity within the family, deference to elders, loyalty to the ruler, and mutual respect between friends.

Another Confucian virtue is *xin,* which involves being trust-worthy, being true to oneself, true to one's moral principles, and hence someone others can trust and depend on. A related value is *cheng,* meaning genuineness or integrity. Confucian learning was aimed at developing the individual's moral strength and character. True Confucians put moral rectitude ahead of temporary expedi-ency. Our idea of "going along to get along" would be anathema to them. When Confucius said, "The true gentleman is not a tool" (*Lunyu,* 2.12), he meant that a morally developed person has his own independent moral standpoint and integrity and does not allow himself to be used by the state (or any organization) without regard for the morality of the situation.

Since political life in East Asia was often corrupt and immoral, the annals of Confucianism are filled with examples of upright men who declined political position rather than compromise their moral beliefs. The Confucian hero is a person who upholds his moral integrity regardless of the consequences for his career, his immediate reputation, or even his personal safety. Confucius said, "Wealth and high rank are what people desire, but they must be forgone if they are not achieved through the Tao" (*Lunyu,* 4.5). Ambition must take second place to considerations of righteous-ness: "If a country lacks the Tao, then it is shameful to have wealth and high rank there" (*Lunyu,* 8.13).

Another classic Confucian virtue is *zhi,* wisdom. Wisdom means the knowledge of Heaven's true pattern, with all that implies for personal conduct and social norms. *The Great Learning* stresses the need to investigate things and extend one's knowledge in order to correctly orient oneself and perfect the ability to function properly in social life. Investigating things means fully fathoming the true inner patterns of things, the principles that govern them.

Confucianism is also a path of self-cultivation. Confucian teach-ers have always placed a major emphasis on education and learn-ing. The *Analects* of Confucius begin, "Is it not delightful to learn and at the proper time recount what one has learned?" Education is necessary to fully develop a person's innate capacity for moral awareness. One must explore the natural patterns of the world at large, and especially the social world, and verify for oneself the correctness of the sages' teachings. Confucius said, "A morally developed person sees an issue from all sides without bias. A petty, selfish person is biased and cannot see an issue from all sides" (*Lunyu*, 2.14).

In the Confucian conception of life, education has an indispensable function in developing personality and preparing people to fulfill their duties to the people around them and to society as a whole. Self-cultivation is the basic starting point: without it, it is impossible to bring proper order to the family, to the local community, and to the wider society.

Confucian education combines book-learning, work on the mind, and application to practical affairs. People need to study the Confucian classics and absorb the wisdom of the sages as well as study past history and appreciate its moral lessons. People also need to look within themselves, to understand and master their own mental impulses, and thus gain self-control over their behavior at the source. Learning must continue amidst practical affairs, as people strive to apply the standards that the classics teach and live up to the examples set by the great Confucians of the past. The goal is to produce people who thoroughly embody the proper norms, so that eventually, like Confucius, they can "follow what the heart desires and not overstep the guidelines" (*Lunyu*, 2.4).

Confucianism contains a well-defined vision of social order and politics. Confucian thinkers emphasized social solidarity as the key to a healthy society. All levels of society must be united by bonds of mutual respect and concern. No society can be strong if the upper and lower classes regard each other with suspicion and hatred. The Confucian classic known as *The Doctrine of the Mean* emphatically states, "Win the confidence of the masses, and you win the state. Lose the confidence of the masses, and you lose the state. Therefore, the superior man is first of all concerned with virtue. If he has virtue, he has the people on his side" (10).

According to the Confucian teaching on politics, it is particularly important for the people at the top to set the proper example and provide moral leadership to society as a whole. "Only those with true human fellow-feeling should be in high position. If people who are not truly humane are in high position, they will spread their evil among the masses" (Mencius, 4a1). If the upper classes use their position to indulge in private gain to the detriment of the livelihood of those below, they destroy the basis of society and forfeit their mandate to rule.

A true ruler is one who wins the people over by satisfying their legitimate needs for justice and material well-being. Confucius said, "To lead a country, [the ruler] must be serious about his business and be trustworthy. He must restrain his expenditures and cherish the people. He must only employ them [for public works] in the proper season [when it does not interfere with their efforts to make a living]" (*Lunyu,* 1.5). Mencius warned that if the common people's livelihood was in doubt, they would be concerned only with basic survival and have no time for proper standards of conduct and moral duty (2a).

Mencius said that a king whose policy was based on true humanity, on human fellow-feeling, would be impossible to resist (1a, 2a). Moral solidarity within society is the key to a nation's strength: "If the lord carries out humane policies, then the common people will love their leaders and be willing to die for them" (1b). Conversely, if the upper classes act only for their own benefit, this will inevitably produce resentment and weaken the society as a whole.

Confucian statecraft teaches that the ruler must choose his officials on the basis of their moral worth, not their hereditary claims to high rank. In a truly Confucian society, those in power must base their claims to legitimacy on their learning and virtue. "When the worthy are in positions of power, and the able are in political office, the state is at peace" (Mencius, 2a). This Confucian ideal was a standing critique of the tendency to aristocratic government and nepotism that long prevailed in East Asia. It supports the notion that rank in society should have a meritocratic basis.

The Confucian tradition canonized the sage rulers of antiquity who were believed to have embodied fully these political ideas. These sage kings ruled by moral force, not by coercion. "He who rules by moral force is like the pole star: it remains in its place and all the other stars do homage to it" (*Lunyu,* 2.1). "If [the ruler] forces people to submit, their minds do not submit: [they give in because] they are not strong enough [to resist]. If the ruler wins people's submission by his virtue, their minds are content: this is real submission" (*Mencius*, 2a).

The sage kings patterned themselves on Heaven and thus were just and impartial. When they resorted to arms, it was always in a just cause. When they picked their helpers and successors, they put talent and moral worth above the claims of hereditary rank. The sage kings were creators, innovators, builders of institutions that served the needs of the people. Knowing of their moral qualities, their wisdom and justice, the people were eager for the sage kings to extend their rule over them: their rule was welcomed "like timely rain." The sage kings were truly "the legates of Heaven."

The Confucian concept of social order and politics thus stands in complete contrast to certain views that hold sway in the modern world. From the Confucian perspective, it is absurd to imagine that a good social order could result from the competitive pursuit of private interests or the unbridled pursuit of gain by the powerful. It is absurd to imagine that a social order based on coercion could in the long run be strong, or even viable. It is absurd to imagine that the best strategy for political leaders is based on deception and intrigue, or that unscrupulous hunger for power and devotion to self-aggrandizement are the marks of a successful leader.

Confucianism was the official ideology of the Chinese Empire for a millennium, but in actual political practice, and in personal life too, Confucian ideals were as often violated as observed.

The relationship between Confucian ideals and East Asian society has always been ambiguous, as ambiguous as the relationship between Christian ideals and Western society. In both civilizations, many people professing allegiance to these ideals behaved in ways that flagrantly contradicted them. Men in power regularly cloaked self-interest with self-righteous claims to incarnate these ideals. Patterns of institutionalized hypocrisy grew and solidified, in which the official defenders of the civilization's ideals ignored and betrayed them in their daily practice.

Certain misconceptions of Confucianism found in the West are related more to the chronic gulf between Confucian ideals and East Asian practice than to the genuine contents of the Confucian teaching itself.

Confucianism is sometimes accused of fostering an attitude of formalism, a concern for outward compliance over inner commitment, a propensity to hide self-interest behind moralistic rhetoric. However prevalent such attitudes might have been in East Asian history, they go against the original inspiration of Confucianism and were criticized through the ages within the tradition under the rubric of "vulgar Confucianism." Confucius himself said, "To carry out rituals without reverence, to go through the motions of mourning without real grief: how can I bear to see such things?" (*Lunyu,* 3.24). Confucian teachers always distinguished between genuine goodness arising from inner moral integrity and a facade of virtue assumed to impress others.

The very fact that Confucianism became institutionalized as the official ideology was fraught with danger for the tradition's high ideals. Men memorized the Confucian classics, not to acquire wisdom but to pass the examinations that opened the way to posts in the bureaucracy, posts that conferred high social status and the best opportunities to get rich. Political life demanded lip-service to Confucian ideals, but ambition was more often served by expediency and compromise. True moral integrity could be very dangerous.

Westerners often assert that Confucianism emphasizes the social to the exclusion of the individual. It is true, of course, that the Confucian tradition does not reflect our modern preoccupation with alienation and our assumption that there is a basic dichotomy between the individual and the society. But throughout history many famous Confucians stood apart from mainstream institutions that they found morally bankrupt and struggled to reconcile personal conscience with the demands of social roles. In actual fact, the Confucian tradition places a major emphasis on the full expression of the individual personality and the maintenance of personal integrity in the face of social pressures. Confucius himself, the exemplar of sagehood, was a man who uncompromisingly went his own way.

Another misconception equates the Confucian tradition with

the authoritarian politics characteristic of East Asia. It is true that loyalty to the ruler is a prime Confucian virtue and that many tyrannical regimes in East Asia have hidden behind a Confucian facade. But this is only half the story.

The Confucian classics insist that the ruling class has a duty to maintain social harmony by following humane policies and insuring the material well-being of those below them. Social disorder is taken as a sign of dereliction of duty by the ruling class: widespread popular discontent is evidence that the ruler has lost Heaven's mandate to rule. Mencius (5a) repeats the classic maxim that Heaven sees and judges the ruler through the eyes of the people. This is the Confucian analogue to the Western *"vox populi, vox Dei."*

The Confucian tradition sharply condemns the politics of tyrants, who rule through coercion and trickery, and reserves political legitimacy for true kings, who rule by moral example and adherence to the Tao. As *The Great Learning* says: "The mandate to rule is not constant. If the moral orientation is good, then it is gained. If the moral orientation is not good, it is lost" (10).

Western commentators beginning with Max Weber have faulted Confucianism for offering no independent moral or religious standpoint over and above the status quo of society from which society could be criticized and reforms proposed. Nothing could be farther from the truth. Beginning with Confucius and Mencius, the leading Confucians always acted as social critics. Throughout history, the most celebrated Confucian heroes were those who had the courage to stand up, often at the risk of their lives, and admonish the men in power for their failure to live up to Confucian moral norms. One of the primary duties of the genuine Confucian was to participate in local and national politics in order to insure that proper norms were honored in public life.

In general, it would make no more sense to blame Confucianism for the defects of the Chinese social order than it would to blame Christianity for the bigotry and genocidal mania that have prevailed so often in the history of the Christian West. It would be more accurate to view both religions as civilizing forces working to make the best of a bad situation and shine some light into the darkness.

Undeniably, both religions were in part co-opted into a pattern of institutionalized hypocrisy. At the same time, both traditions held the potential to inspire sincere believers to actively seek means to bring their ideals to life. Both traditions preserved in their classics a kernel of wisdom and insight into human life and the conditions under which it could flourish.

Volumes could be written about the history of Confucianism, tracing its initial inspiration, its inner dynamic, its interactions with the Chinese imperial state, its philosophical encounters with Taoism and Buddhism, its spread into Korea, Vietnam, and Japan, its adaptation to the modern world. Here my only purpose is to point out certain landmark events in the history of the tradition that are directly relevant for understanding the Confucian teachings translated in the present work.

In the long history of Confucianism in China, three periods of intense creativity stand out.

The first period extended from about 500 to 200 B.C.E. and was marked by intensifying warfare among the various states that ruled the different regions of China. This was an era when all aspects of social life and custom came in for intense rethinking, the era that produced the classical philosophies of China. This period includes the seminal teaching mission of Confucius himself (d. 479 B.C.E.); the activities of his immediate disciples who spread the tradition across the many states that then comprised China; the composition of the Confucian classics, like *The Great Learning, The Doctrine of the Mean,* and the Confucian layer of the *I Ching;* the work of Mencius (d. 289 B.C.E.), the great reviver of the Confucian message; and the work of Xunzi (d. 238 B.C.E.), who attempted to codify and systematize Confucian philosophy. This was the period when the basic axioms of the Confucian tradition were set forth and Confucian views began to win a wide following.

The second peak of Confucian creativity was in the Song dynasty, during the eleventh and twelfth centuries C.E. Many Song thinkers concentrated on applying Confucian principles of statecraft to solving the pressing problems of society, like growing inequality and the breakdown of social solidarity. The great

Confucian philosophers of this period were of the opinion that since the time of Mencius, the Confucian tradition had become moribund, declining into lackluster formalism and rote learning. Leading Song Confucians, like Zhou Dunyi and Zhang Zai, Cheng Hao and Cheng Yi, saw themselves as renewing Confucianism by reestablishing a direct link with the original message of Confucius and Mencius. They insisted that true Confucians must embody the wisdom of the classics in their own lives and strive to live up to the examples of the sages. Their work led to a renewed emphasis among Confucians on personal self-cultivation and the attainment of wisdom.

Viewed from the outside, the Buddhist influences on this new Confucianism are apparent. Quiet sitting modeled on Zen meditation became a major part of Confucian self-cultivation. There was a lot of talk about mind, about curbing desires, about reuniting the human mind with the primordial mind of the Tao. Song Confucians stressed the innate human potential for sagehood, much as Buddhists emphasized the innate potential for enlightenment in all people.

Much equivocation accompanied this infusion of Buddhist influences. Some Song Confucians openly admitted their affinity to Buddhism and argued that Buddhism and Confucianism were perfectly compatible, citing selected passages from the Confucian classics to prove their point. Other Song Confucians took great pains to point out what they saw as crucial differences between the two traditions and insisted that only Confucianism provided a comprehensive plan for both self-cultivation and correct social action. Among the Confucians who rejected Buddhism was Zhu Xi (d. 1200), whose views became the standard of orthodoxy on the official examinations from the fourteenth century onward.

The third great period of Confucian creativity came in the sixteenth and early seventeenth centuries, the later half of the Ming dynasty.

This was an era of intense change in Chinese society. The economy was becoming more and more commercialized. Trade and handicraft manufacturing flourished in the cities and towns. In many areas peasants specialized in growing cash crops for the market and bought their food. Middlemen proliferated. Little by

Introduction

little, serfs were freed and labor obligations were commuted to money payments. Farmers came to pay their taxes in silver instead of grain. In more and more regions of the country, the personal bonds between tenants and landowners were replaced by monetary relations. Labor became more mobile, as country people left the land to work in the towns or engage in trade.

Chinese culture was in great ferment in the sixteenth century. A rich literature in the vernacular language appeared for the first time, reflecting the lives and concerns of the non-elite city people. There was a brisk business in the printing and selling of books appealing to popular tastes. These books, though written to entertain, reflect the growing confusion of values and beliefs. They show people expressing skepticism about religion, cynicism about personal relations, and even disillusion with the pursuit of profit, status, and pleasure. Satires poke fun at worldly Buddhist monks and nuns and hypocritical Confucian gentlemen. The painting of the period suggests a world under strain, its underlying structures being brought to the surface and contorted without being able to reach a new synthesis.

This period was also a time of growing political tension. The dynasty (founded in 1368) was growing old. Capricious emperors, reared in luxury, refused to play their appointed role in the political system and withdrew into private pursuits. The government was left in the hands of rival cliques of bureaucrats and powerful eunuchs acting in the name of the emperor. Factionalism and intrigue intensified. The official career in government service for which cultured gentlemen were trained became ever more hazardous and morally compromising. Among the common people, there were more and more rent riots, peasant mutinies, and millenarian conspiracies. *Tales of the Water Margin,* one of the most popular novels of the period, features as its heroes common men who fight back against oppressive, conniving, corrupt officials.

This later Ming era was a fertile period for religion in China.

Taoism maintained its perennial vitality, making its presence widely felt in popular religion and literature and folklore. Its adherents ranged from wishful thinkers seeking the secrets of health and long life, to adepts who had mastered the fusion of primordial energy and action in the temporal world. The great masterpiece *Journey to the West* gives some indication of the sophistication and subtlety of the Taoist view of the contemporary human condition and shows consummate skill in communicating profound observations through humor, satire, and fable.

Buddhism experienced a revival in the sixteenth century. The Ming laws restricting contacts between Buddhist monks and nuns and the common people fell into disuse, along with the legal limitations on the number of monks and nuns and Buddhist temples. Many temples were rebuilt, and much Buddhist literature was gathered together and reprinted in easily accessible book form. Zen retained its prestige in intellectual circles and spread its influence among Confucian gentlemen. Among all classes in China, Pure Land Buddhist practice was widespread.

Many religious people in Ming China advocated a synthesis of Taoism, Confucianism, and Buddhism, and "merging the Three Teachings into one" became a major trend. Many people invoked Taoist, Confucian, and Buddhist values side by side with no sense of contradiction or incongruity.

Confucianism rose to the challenges of social and cultural change in sixteenth-century China with a new wave of creativity and innovativeness. Many Confucian teachers became concerned with spreading the classic teachings of the sages and traveled widely, giving lectures to diverse audiences. Leading Confucians founded teaching academies and trained disciples to spread their new views.

By this time, the stream of Confucianism associated with the name of Zhu Xi had hardened into an orthodoxy. For some it still retained the ability to inspire genuine self-cultivation. But for many others, it had become a mechanical exercise, a body of thought that had to be memorized in order to pass the official exams, but meant little beyond that.

The teachings and personal presence of the statesman, thinker, and teacher Wang Yangming (d. 1529) gave new impetus to Confucian thought in the sixteenth century. Whereas Zhu Xi had stressed the immutable normative patterns that must order personal and social life, Wang Yangming shifted the focus to the innate human capacity for moral judgment. Whereas Zhu Xi's worldview had a static, closed quality, Wang Yangming's teaching appeared more dynamic, more open-ended. By getting in touch with his innate moral knowledge, the person has a way to keep his moral bearings and correctly guide his actions through all sorts of changing, novel situations. Wang Yangming taught that by refining and perfecting one's innate capacity for moral awareness, it would be possible to reach a level of unerring spontaneity of response and accuracy of judgment in all situations.

Already in his own lifetime, Wang Yangming exerted a tremendous influence on contemporary Confucianism, arousing great interest in his teachings and also considerable opposition. He had many dedicated followers who made it their business to spread his ideas: men who wrote, lectured, founded academies, and attracted disciples of their own. Some became active in popular education, trying to extend the Confucian message beyond the educated elite by lecturing to people in all walks of life. Thus the Wang Yangming school and its offshoots became the creative mainstream of Confucian thinking in the later Ming period.

How does the story end? With the conquest of China by Manchu invaders in the middle decades of the seventeenth century, the situation changed profoundly. A reaction set in, and Confucian gentlemen under the new dynasty repudiated the openness and originality of Ming thought. Not until the Western invasion shattered the old order in the nineteenth century did China again embark upon such a momentous age of intellectual and cultural questioning.

In our century Chinese thought has passed through another age of fluidity and another age of rigid orthodoxy. It is worth remembering that the ideas of the avant-garde of the Ming period would still be avant-garde in the Chinese world of today: spontaneity, freedom of conscience, self-realization, the right to one's own opinion.

The plan of this book is as follows:
First, passages from the works of several leading Confucians from the fifteenth and early sixteenth centuries who represent the best of the tradition of thought deriving from the Song Confucians, like the Cheng brothers and Zhu Xi, the kind of Confucianism that held sway before the impact of Wang Yangming.

Next, selections from the writings of three Confucians of the so-called Sweet Spring school, with careers spanning the sixteenth century, whose point of view is a continuation of the Cheng-Zhu tradition but in certain ways shows more openness.

Then, for the major part of the book, the teachings of Wang Yangming and his followers. The Wang Yangming school deserves the most space as the creative leading edge of the Confucian thought of its time.

Finally, selections from a trio of thinkers who do not fall into any particular school of thought, as a token of the diversity of Ming Confucianism.

These selections are drawn from Huang Zongxi's pioneering seventeenth-century work *Studies of Ming Confucians (Ming Ru Xue-an)*. In the case of Wang Yangming himself, I also used the *Chuanxilu*, a collection of his teachings put together by his disciples. In selecting excerpts to translate, I have looked for passages that reveal the quintessential concerns of the tradition and at the same time have the most practical interest and universal appeal.

The table on page xxv, for those who may be interested, gives the literary names of each of the teachers represented in this book, as well as the volume of the *Ming Ru Xue-an* from which their passages were chosen. With the exception of Wang Yangming, the teachers are identified in this book by their personal rather than their literary names.

Personal Name	Literary Name	Volume in *Ming Rue Xue-an*
Wu Yubi	Kangzhai	1
Hu Juren	Jingzhai	2
Xue Xuan	Jingxuan	7
Xia Shangpu	Dongyan	4
Lü Nan	Jingye	8
Zhan Ruoshui	Ganyuan	37
Hong Yuan	Jueshan	39
Feng Congwu	Shaoxu	41
Wang Shouren	Yangming	10
Wang Ji	Longqi	12
Qian Dehong	Xushan	11
Wang Gen	Xinzhai	32
Zou Shouyi	Dongkuo	16
Ouyang De	Nanye	17
Nie Bao	Shuangjiang	17
Luo Hongxian	Nian-an	18
Lui Wenmin	Liangfeng	19
Chen Jiuchuan	Mingshui	19
Wan Tingyan	Simo	21
Zhou Chong	Jing-an	25
Zhu Dezhi	Jinzhai	25
Xue Yingqi	Fangshan	25
Zha Shengduo	Yizhai	25
Tang Shunzhi	Jingshan	26
Xu Jie	Cunzhai	27
Yang Yusun	Youyin	27
Luo Rufang	Jinqi	34
Geng Dingxiang	Tiantai	35
Xu Yongjian	Luyuan	14
Zhang Yuanbian	Yanghe	15
Wang Shihuai	Tangnan	20
Zou Yuanbiao	Nangao	23
Jiao Hong	Danyuan	35
Zhu Shilu	Wugong	35
Luo Qinshun	Zheng-an	47
Li Zhong	Guping	53
Lü Kun	Xinwu	54

WU YUBI

Wu Yubi (1391–1469) was the son of a high official, the head of the National Academy, where the imperial princes and the sons of courtiers and high officials were educated. As a teenager Wu Yubi read Zhu Xi's account of the Song dynasty Confucian philosophers and became intent on following the Confucian Path. To his father's dismay, he gave up studies directed purely toward the offical examinations.

After serving briefly in the capital, Wu Yubi returned home for good. When traveling in his home area he dressed simply so that no one would know he was the son of a high official. He supported himself by farming and personally took part in the farm labor. Many disciples gathered around him, and he made them work in the fields by his side.

In his old age Wu Yubi was summoned to the capital by the emperor and offered a position as tutor to the crown prince. Many important people in the capital sought Wu Yubi out, but others ridiculed his insistence on classic forms of etiquette. Wu Yubi steadfastly refused any imperial appointment, and finally he was given a pension and allowed to return home.

You must properly manage your mind and make it sparkling clean and always alert. Only this is good enough. This is the work of being reverent in order to correct your inner state.

Alas! If you are not reverent, then you will not be straightforward, and if you are not straightforward, everything will be ruined. Should you not fear this?

If you do not have the time to check up on yourself rigorously day and night, then what free time do you have to check up on others? To be strict in blaming others and lax in regulating yourself: is this not to be warned against? [*The Great Learning* prescribes] making your virtue shine and renewing the people. Though these are not two different endeavors, if your own virtue

1

has not been made bright and you are in a hurry to renew the people, not only have you lost the proper order of priority, but you will not be able to be effective in renewing the people. You will make trouble in vain and only achieve selfish aims.

To be rich and high-ranked without becoming dissolute, to be poor and lowly and still be happy: if a man can reach this level, he is outstanding.

If you have not reached the Tao of Heaven, if you have not reached sagehood, you cannot be called an accomplished person. This is why the outstanding people of the past worked so hard all their lives.

In all matters it is necessary to reach decisions based on righteousness. To calculate profit and loss is wrong.

In the midst of poverty, low rank, misfortune, and difficult circumstances, you must manage to take a firm stand, overcome crudity and heedlessness, and make your mind and nature pure. You must not resent Heaven above or be aggrieved with people below. With things and self both forgotten, recognize only the true pattern and that's all.

If you do not fulfill the Tao to the very last detail, then you are cutting yourself off from Heaven.

If you place your body in the realm of equanimity and noncontention, and let your mind roam in the territory of evenness and nondisturbance, and water them every day with the fair words and fine deeds of the sage worthies, then you are sure to progress.

To nurture this mind, the most important work in everyday activities is not to be overcome by things.

Worldly Wisdom

.

I took a carefree walk outside and then came home. Master Zhu Xi said, "Harmony and happiness are just not having any concerns in your mind." How true these words are! In recent days my body and mind have been a bit more tranquil: again it seems I have made some progress.

When a profound person struggles against petty people, not only is he unable to win, but actually he *should not* win [because he should not even be struggling with them].

I have made a little progress in my study of the *I Ching*. My only regret is that my energy is diminishing [with age] and I do not have much time [left]. So I must make as much effort as I can and finish the rest of my life on this task.

Today I contemplated the principle of being at peace whatever circumstances are encountered. The sense of rest is still with me. This purpose does not admit any slackening. How could I get sick and tired of things due to old age?

I have been talking with students for a long time. In general I urge them to nurture and tend the basic root of the self and not let any ideas of seeking gain sprout up.

Sitting quitely alone [meditating] is not hard. What is hard is living on a broad scale and responding to the world at large.

Whenever things are hurried, they will be spoiled.

Do not damage true mind with false thoughts or injure the original energy with transient energies.

Someone else may treat me with a covetous and deceitful attitude, but I will deal with him using the essential body of the true great light.

To engage in learning to the point that you feel no rancor toward people is the perfection of learning. I have heard this described, but I have not yet seen anyone [who really accomplished it].

There is no time, there is no place that is not for the work [of self-cultivation].

Though the myriad transformations are confusing, each has a fixed pattern for responding to it.

HU JUREN

Hu Juren (1434–1484) came from a prosperous farming family. From an early age he was intent on Confucian learning. After meeting Wu Yubi, he gave up plans to study for the official exams and pursued learning untainted by worldly ambition. He traveled through the neighboring provinces calling on learned men and giving lectures. He returned to his home area, where his disciples built him a teaching studio. The story goes that Hu Juren was always very strict with himself and set out a course of study for each day. He checked up on his progress by keeping a ledger of what he learned and the mistakes he made. He did not follow popular customs, but kept to the ancient norms. He lived by farming and paid no attention to his poverty, preferring to devote himself to the Tao.

To be aware when your mind is going astray is indeed a good thing. Then you must focus your attention and gather it in and not let it run off anymore. This is the meditation work of taking charge and preserving the mind of reverence. If your mind does not know where it is, and everything is vague and uncertain, what kind of meditation is this?

Full knowledge of the true pattern does not have a single starting point, and it is not attained in only one way. Some get it from the books they read. Some get it from lectures. Some get it while thinking and pondering. Some get it while doing things. Though many get it from reading books, to get it from lectures is faster, to get it by thinking and pondering is deeper, and to get it by doing things is the most genuine.

Confucius taught people to proceed in their conduct from integrity and trustworthiness and sincerity and reverence, to be able to gather in their minds when they went astray and nurture for themselves their virtuous nature. Mencius expressed the concept of searching for lost mind in order to teach people. But people did not hold firmly to this as a model in their cultivation work. Therefore Master Cheng in his teachings emphasized reverence.

Once the human mind goes astray, truth, the true pattern of the Tao, is lost. Once the human mind is gathered in, the true pattern of the Tao is there.

Adhere correctly to righteousness, and do not calculate gain. If those engaged in learning use this principle to establish their minds, then there will be greatness and illuminaton. Those who fulfill this principle are pure Confucians. To extend it and put it into practice is the policy of a pure monarch.

A true king is one who does not interfere when things remain in their proper pattern. One who calculates what is in his own private selfish interest is inclined to tyranny.

People may uphold reverence, but they also must be permeated with the true pattern of righteousness. Only then will they attain the joyousness of this mind. If not, they will just be stubbornly holding onto something.

Reverence is the path for preserving and nurturing [the mind of the Tao]. It runs through [the process] from beginning to end. As the saying goes, nurturing [the mind of the Tao] requires the use of reverence, and making progress in learning is a matter of extending knowledge. That is, before you know, you must first nurture this mind: only then can you extend knowledge. It is also said: having recognized this true pattern, use truthfulness and reverence to preserve it. Thus, after extending knowledge, it is still necessary to preserve and nurture it: only then will it not be lost. In sum, the work of extending knowledge is intermittent; the work of preserving and nurturing [the mind of the Tao] never stops.

The mind becoming purified and illuminated is the result of reverence.

If you can really take reverence as your ruling principle, then you will automatically be free of miscellaneous thoughts. In every case, those who want to block off thoughts have not yet perfected reverence.

Reverence is an exercise in control. It is not the case that there is some separate work of controlling and preserving [the mind] beyond reverence. Investigating things is extending knowledge. It is not the case that there is some separate work of extending knowledge beyond investigating things.

The means by which to manage this mind is the true pattern. The means by which we are equipped with the true pattern is mind. Therefore, where the true pattern is correct, mind is at peace, and where mind is preserved, the true pattern is there. It is not only this way in ourselves, but also in other people. When what we do is in accord with the true pattern, other people are transformed by the influence of this and cooperate. It is not only this way with people, but with all things. If what we do is in accord with the true pattern, all things will get their due.

These days when people study, many do so for the sake of reputation. In this way, when they study, they have already departed from the Tao. They waste a lifetime of effort and can never attain the Tao.

If affairs are handled by intellect and calculation [instead of moral norms], people will not go along, and private interests will diverge.

Even though there are affairs in the world that are difficult to deal with, if you deal with them following the true pattern, without calculations of profit and loss, then your fundamental mind will be serene of itself. If you do not adopt the true pattern of righteousness as your guiding principle, when you encounter affairs that are hard to deal with, they will become even harder to handle.

The mark of the Confucian is to handle affairs, not by intellectual calculations, but by following the true pattern of Heaven.

Outside the way of the true king there is no smooth path. Outside humanity and righteousness there is no accomplishment or benefit.

To be upright and correct and serious and proper is where reverence starts. To keep your attention focused and alert is where reverence continues. To be unified no matter what the circumstances and be profoundly clear and pure is reverence without interruptions. To be awake and undimmed, illuminated and undisturbed, is reverence taking effect.

Reverence includes both movement and stillness. To sit quietly and be upright and solemn is reverence. To follow along with events, investigating them and extending your most scrupulous efforts, is also reverence. Reverence encompasses both inner and outer. When your demeanor is serious and correct, that is reverence. When your mind-ground is profoundly clear and pure, that is reverence.

It is impossible to extend knowledge without being in a state of reverence. Reverence is its basis.

Coarseness of mind is most damaging to all affairs. Coarseness of mind is when reverence is not perfected.

The true pattern of Heaven has good but not evil. Evil is born from going beyond [the true pattern] or not reaching [the true pattern]. The true nature of humanity has good but not evil. Evil is born from our endowment of physical energy and our material desires.

As soon as there is confusion or laziness, the true pattern of righteousness is automatically lost.

XUE XUAN

Xue Xuan (1389–1464) was the son of an official in charge of local education. Xue Xuan himself won the highest degree in 1421 and embarked upon a career as an official. Running afoul of the most powerful man in the government, the eunuch Liu Qin, he narrowly escaped execution in 1443. He was also active in the defense of Beijing against the Mongol invaders in 1450 and in famine relief efforts in the Yangzi valley.

As a provincial education inspector, Xue Xuan promoted the works of Zhu Xi; he reportedly thought that Zhu Xi had said it all, and all that was left to do was to put his teachings into practice.

Among the essentials of learning, none is more crucial than movement and stillness. If movement and stillness accord with what is proper, this is Heaven's true pattern. If they do not accord with what is proper, this is human desire.

When movement and stillness are in accord with Heaven's true pattern, this is the Tao.

That by which the transformations of *yin* and *yang* take place is surely the activity of the true pattern. But the true pattern itself is fixed and does not change: it is constant.

The former Confucians said, "What is in things is the true pattern. What deals with things is righteousness." The humaneness of the monarch, the reverence of his ministers, the compassion of the father, the filial behavior of the sons: these are all examples of the true pattern in things. To manage with these so that each gets what is proper to it is righteousness in dealing with things.

In the things you do every day, you must be fully aware of what human fellow-feeling is, what moral duty is, what proper forms of behavior are, what wisdom is. When you have done this for a long time, you will see the Tao clearly.

For twenty years I have dealt with anger, and I have still not managed to dissolve it away completely. Thus I know that controlling oneself is difficult.

9

.

The work of fully realizing mind is entirely a matter of knowing true nature and knowing Heaven above. This is because true nature is the true pattern, and Heaven is where the pattern comes from. If a person can know true nature and know Heaven, then he is clear about all the true patterns of the world, and the true pattern of this mind runs through everything.

Broad learning is knowing this true pattern. Keeping to proper norms of behavior is carrying out this true pattern.

If your sincerity cannot move people, you should blame yourself. If you cannot influence people, it is always because your sincerity is not perfect.

To be deep, serious, tranquil, composed, generous, relaxed: this is the foundation for advancing in virtue.

To manage people who are difficult to handle, do not use a sharp voice and a stern face. Talk over with them what is right and wrong, and compare advantages and disadvantages.

If people are capable of not daring to be negligent when they speak and act and of dealing with all things properly, then the vast flooding energy [which Mencius spoke of] is generated spontaneously.

You must do away with your old habits and start fresh. Master Zhang Zai said, "Wash away your old opinions, and let new ideas come." Once in the predawn hours I recognized why my virtue was not making much progress. It was just because I was wrapped up in old habits and had not been able to get rid of them. Thus, though I did good, the good was not complete, and though I got rid of evil, the evil was not totally gone. From then on, I have worked to cut away old habits, and I seek to accord with the Tao in every word and every act. Otherwise I would not be a [real] man.

If a single thought is wrong, immediately stop it. If a single act is false, immediately change it.

If you look up and down at the infinite expanse of Heaven and Earth, you will know how great the Tao is and feel how small the world is.

The most essential point in the work is to accord with the rules of Heaven in everything day and night, in drinking and eating, in sexual relations, in how you dress, in how you act and speak, in how you deal with situations and receive people. The Tao does not lie beyond this.

You must realize that you yourself, along with all things, came forth from the creative transformations of *yin* and *yang*. Then you will know that the myriad things of Heaven and Earth have one essential substance.

It is a great misfortune for those engaged in learning to take the sayings of the sages as mere verbal exercises.

If your will moves your vital energy, then you mostly act for truth. If your vital energy moves your will, then you mostly act for desires.

If you are reverent, then the dregs are dissolved, and nothing can overcome your greatness. If you are not reverent, then vulgar greed sprouts, and if you do not overcome it, you become small.

Master Cheng's saying "Our real nature is the true pattern" is enough to settle all the doubts in all the arguments about our real nature since ancient times.

The merciful and compassionate mind of humans is identical to the mind of Heaven and Earth that lovingly gives life to beings.

As soon as you gather in body and mind, you are abiding in reverence. As soon as you ponder the principles of moral duty, you are getting to the bottom of the true pattern. These two depend on each other: neither one can be absent.

In the first stages of learning, we see abiding in reverence and fully fathoming the true pattern as two separate things. After learning for a long time, we can see that when abiding in reverence, we are reverent because we are preserving the true pattern, and when fully fathoming the true pattern, we are reverent because we are investigating the true pattern. It seems that these are two things, but really they are one.

Reading books to fortify this mind is like taking medicine to disperse an illness. Though the illness may not be removed [at first], if you always make the power of the medicine prevail, the illness will naturally weaken. Though the mind may not yet be stabilized [at first], if you always deeply savor books, the mind will naturally ripen. After a long time, the illness, which has been weakened, will be totally gone, and the mind, which has been ripening, will be completely transformed.

When affairs are many and complex, our minds must have their own guiding principle. We should not be moved by the vexations of affairs.

All times and all places are occasions to work on learning.

All things with forms reveal the formless true pattern. As it is said, not one of them is not a perfect teaching.

For all human minds, there is that which makes them secure and that which makes them insecure. What makes them secure is the true pattern of moral duty. What makes them insecure is human desire. When selfish interest prevails and they cannot control themselves, then they think that insecurity is security.

People seek the Tao within themselves. Little do they know that outside themselves all is the Tao.

As soon as you accomplish something, to want people to know it: this is the epitome of shallowness.

If the true pattern is clearly understood, then the mind is stable.

If the true pattern is clearly understood, then you see the myriad things in Heaven and Earth all at peace in their proper place.

There is nothing in the world without the true pattern and no such thing as the true pattern without things.

In whatever you do, seek to accord with the true pattern right then and there. Do not say, "Today I will play false like this, but tomorrow I will reform." If you play false in one thing, all the rest will be false too.

If you cut off thoughts of plotting for gain and planning for success, your mind will be transcendent and without entanglements.

Do not look at or listen to or say or do anything that is not proper: this is controlling yourself. Where what you look at and listen to and say and do accords with the true pattern, this is returning to the proper norm.

If the words and principles you use when you teach people are too lofty, you give them nothing they can rely on.

Always keep your mind on the true pattern of righteousness. After a long time, you will gradually understand it clearly. If you keep your mind on idle things, then the true pattern of righteousness will seem more and more obscure to you.

Even with sincere will and energetic practice, if you do not know the Tao, you will end up shallow.

The true pattern in one mind is fundamentally no different from the true pattern in the myriad things. Only the sages can use the true pattern in one mind to comprehend the true pattern in the myriad things. This is because they have in pure form the impartial fairness of Heaven's true pattern.

There is no place the Tao is not present, so there is no place we must not act diligently.

If miscellaneous thoughts are reduced, we gradually approach the Tao.

Whenever the mind has false thoughts, control it with the words of the classics and the sages.

XIA SHANGPU

Xia Shangpu received the highest degree in 1511 and in time rose high in the bureaucracy. In his teaching activities, he emphasized the value of reverence, the attitude of seriousness and respect in dealing with all situations.

For students to nurture this mind, they must be like fish swimming in water to succeed.

As soon as it is raised up, it is the true pattern of Heaven. As soon as it is let down, it is human desire.

The mind of a morally developed person has no room for the slightest evil, any more than dust can be [comfortably] put in a person's eye.

Those engaged in learning must gather together their spirit. It is like a brazier full of fire. If the embers are gathered together, the flames blaze up; if they are scattered, then it goes dark.

The true pattern of the Tao is something sweet. Master Zhu Xi's "Poem to Instruct the Immature" says: "In action, your mind is at peace, in thought you attain / The sweet taste fills your mouth to overflowing." This is no metaphor.

Do not ask whether this mind is quiet or not. Just ask whether this mind is reverent or not. With reverence, the mind is automatically quiet.

Reverence is not an external decoration: it is the way our hearts must be. When we are reverent, our minds are at peace. As soon as we abandon [reverence], this mind is not at peace. What is called reverence is what in common parlance is spoken of as "always mobilizing the spirit."

When there is harmony between the true pattern and our vital energy, this is the vast flood of energy [praised by Mencius]. When our vital energy goes against the true pattern, this is transient alien energy.

Righteousness comes forth from within, like a sharp knife or sharp ax cutting through, making everything be as it should. This is concentrated righteousness. If you work to put on a false facade and follow along with externals, this is an outer layer of righteousness.

The intent of Heaven and Earth is to give life to beings. If people can have as their intent to aid other people and benefit beings, then they are in accord with the intent of Heaven and Earth, and they deserve to receive blessings from Heaven.

True humanity is a virtue of the mind: it is like the kernel of a fruit. If there is the slightest selfishness inside, then [true humanity] is spoiled. How then can it come to life and develop in the outer world?

Do not put on a facade of clever speech and a winning manner. If you have the slightest intention of gaining favor from people, this is clever speech and a winning manner. To be aware of this and be careful about it is a method for becoming truly humane.

Students must first recognize the true pattern. When planting grain, if you do not recognize its seed, how can you be sure you will not mistake grass seed for seed grain? [If you plant grass seed by mistake], then even though you do your utmost to nurture it,

16

it will just grow to be grass. In recent generations there have been Confucians who try hard their whole lives but end up slipping into deviant schools of thought without realizing it: they are guilty of not recognizing the true pattern.

"The Tao is like a great highway: how could it be hard to recognize?" These words give people a place to start. In your daily activities, serve your parents like this, serve your elders like this, talk like this, act like this, deal with people like this. There is a road and a proper measure for every stituation. The true great highway is like this. It's just that when people encounter situations they get confused and make blunders. If in every situation they would be willing to enter into careful thought, then [they would discover that] in their minds a rule for how they should act is there by itself. What need is there to search elsewhere?

If you crave wealth and high rank and abhor poverty and low rank, whether you succeed or not, this attitude of craving and abhorring has already separated you from true humanity.

The mind must be active. In your daily activities always place your mind on the true pattern of righteousness. This is preserving the mind. To preserve the mind it is not necessary to sit cross-legged with eyes closed all day long in silence without any mental activity.

Contemporary people know only about profit. When they speak of humanity and righteousness, they are sure to ridicule them and consider them unrealistic. Little do they know that there is harm in profit. If you devote yourself to humanity and right-eousness, then, without seeking profit, everything will automatically be advantageous.

If the head of a family honors profit, then the whole family will honor profit. Because of this, fathers and sons and elder and younger brothers will struggle against each other to get advantage and will cut each other up, and the family is sure to fall to ruin and come to an end.

If the head of the family respects righteousness, this will cause the whole family to respect righteousness. Because of this, fathers will be compassionate toward their sons, and the sons will be filial toward their fathers. Elder brothers will be friends with their younger brothers, and younger brothers will respect their elder brothers. No one will be talking about what good fortune may come to their door. They will just rest content with the harmonious atmosphere they already have at home. How can profit compare to this?

LÜ NAN

Lü Nan (1479–1542) took first place in the highly competitive examinations for the highest degree in 1501. He was a man of uncompromising integrity, and consequently his official career was anything but smooth. Three times he was driven from office for taking a moral stand on controversial issues and going against the wishes of men at the top.

Lü Nan was known as a talented writer and composed commentaries on the Confucian classics and the works of the Song Confucians. Though Lü Nan favored the Cheng-Zhu style of Xue Xuan and Zhan Ruoshui, he also knew the thought of Wang Yangming. He was able to use his influence to shield his mentor Zhan Ruoshui from persecution and also to block attempts to ban the works of Wang Yangming.

Throughout his career Lü Nan was active in lecturing on learning and founded academies for talented students from among the people.

Guangzu said, "When plants get rain, they live and grow. The result is very quick. Why do some people not flourish when they get teaching?"

Master Lü said, "Because their inner minds are not genuine. It is like when seeds are infested with weevils or spoiled by dampness: how hard it is for them to sprout!"

Someone said, "In forming friendships, in managing a family, in conducting oneself in the world, we cannot achieve goodness in all things. This is the worst difficulty for people."

Master Lü said, "In this, one must have an attitude of sympathy to do well. If one can be sympathetic, then one knows how to make the proper distinctions and handle things accordingly. For example, if one's wife and concubines are ignorant and one's brothers are unworthy, one should not say they are wrong. This is the path of harmonizing knowledge with human fellow-feeling."

Someone asked, "Why are there so many points of disagreement among those today who lecture on learning?"

Master Lü said, "It is because there are disagreements that they lecture on learning. If they all thought alike, then what would be the use of lecturing? Thus, when employing people to bring political order to the people, we should not always seek sameness. If we sought the same opinions in everyone, then people skilled at currying favor and flattery would come to the fore."

To see what is good and be willing to carry it out: this is strength. To drown in current fashions and material desires: this is weakness.

When Master Lü heard that a certain student had gone to seek to become a disciple of a powerful, high-ranking man, he said: "When men wait at the gates of the powerful imperial favorites, they lose what they should hold to. Therefore I teach people to be content with poverty and keep working [at self-cultivation], to plant their feet firmly and not be moved."

Worldly Wisdom

I have heard that in the old days an official sought a meeting with Master Wang Zhang-an by saying to him, "I came west, first to see the Yellow River, second to see Mount Hua, and third to see you, Master."

Master Wang said, "If you do not perform your official duties well, then even if you see these three things, it will not help matters." How lofty Master Wang was: he did not accept flattery.

Cultivation does not necessarily have to be done [in retreat] in the mountains and forests. It can also be done in cities and at court.

In the old days the monk Zhongnan practiced cultivation for thirty years, doing nothing but meditation. A monk said to him, "You have practiced stillness for a long time, [it is time to go out in the world]." Together they went to the brothel section of Chang-an. When they got there they saw enticing creatures wearing makeup and rouge. Zhongnan's mind was moved, and in one day he spoiled the work of the previous thirty years.

From this we can see that it is indeed necessary to study [not only in sheltered retreats, but also] in complex, colorful, noisy, chaotic situations.

Daqi asked, "Is there a way to seek happiness?"

Master Lü said, "Each person should pick out what entangles him and get rid of it totally. Then naturally both mind and body will be at peace. What I mean by 'what entangles you' is not necessarily coarse and evil things like sensory pleasures and greed for gain. It could be calligraphy or composing poetry. [What entangles you] is everything that you are overly fond of. Master Cheng said, 'Books are the things closest at hand for Confucian scholars, but if they are too attached to them, one can see that the scholars have lost their true purpose.' "

The younger brother of a powerful state minister was passing through Shaanxi. He said to Duishan, "When I return to the capital, I will speak with my older brother and recommend that he employ you."

Duishan laughed and said, "I am hardly the sort of man who would win fame at the hands of such a man."

Master Lü said, "This man can indeed be called a noble-minded scholar."

Master Lü met Lin Ying and saw how he radiated equanimity. He pointed this out to Daqi and said, "If a man is equanimous while moving and while at rest, and his words are temperate and fitting, not only does he accord in this way with Heaven's true pattern, but those who behold him respect and cherish him. This is learning. Those who study cannot be without this atmosphere of equanimity. They must first have it within them."

Shiyao asked, "Where should we gather in lost mind?"

Master Lü said, "You must gather it in where you lost it. Then you will recover it without going far."

Master Lü said to his students, "If we desire to be truly humane, then true humanity will come. These days those who lecture on learning are very lofty and remote. I make a pact with all you students to start from the basic studies. You must see the true pattern of the Tao wherever you are: the truth of serving your parents, the truth of how you deal with your clansmen and wives and children, the truth of how to treat servants and bondsmen. Using these truths, you can confront the spirits, you can face the sun and moon, and you can enlighten those who come to study. All this is acting from what is genuine."

Daqi said, "With true humanity, it is indeed a matter of fully developing it."

Master Lü said, "That is so."

Someone asked about learning, saying, "[I understand that] it is only necessary to correct oneself. Confucius said, 'I do not resent Heaven above or mankind below. The one who knows me is

21

Heaven. If I seek to be known by mankind, then the road becomes narrow. Where should one seek Heaven? Just in winning over the people. Winning over the people is winning over Heaven.' *The Classic of History* says, 'Heaven sees through our people seeing. Heaven hears through our people hearing.' I do not understand."

Master Lü said, "You base [learning] in [your own] single mind and make it take effect in [your own] single body. [The proper course is] to apply it to your extended family, then extend it to your neighbors; only then do you consummate it in political affairs. There is nowhere it cannot go. In all affairs you must have human fellow-feeling to spare and a sense of duty that is not too excessive: then everyone will be won over."

Shao asked how to teach about innate moral knowledge.

Master Lü said, "When the sages taught people, they always transformed people based on how the people were. For example, when Yan Yuan asked about true humanity, Confucius told him about controlling oneself and returning to proper norms of behavior. Zhong Gong he told about reverence and forgiveness. Fan Chi he told to live respectfully, to handle things with reverence, and to be forgiving toward people. In general, he let people progress in accordance with their dispositions and the extent reached by their power to learn. He never rigidly confined them to one single method. When contemporary Confucians teach people, they never take into account their natural endowment or their level of learning. They stress a few ideas and insist that people follow them. Isn't this one-sided?"

Master Lü told his students, "You are good only if you never change, whether you are in private or in public, whether you meet frustration or success. People these days are one person when they are in public in front of a lot of people and another person when they are living alone in retirement. They are one person when they are facing the rich and noble and another person with the poor and lowly. The only pure ones are those who are unchanged whatever meets their eyes."

When students get lazy and self-indulgent, there is always a lack of human fellow-feeling. If there is human fellow-feeling, after that, you never slack off.

He Yanren said that the way Master Yangming taught people using [the idea of] innate knowledge had greatly benefited students.

Master Lü said, "This [idea of innate knowledge] is a generalized teaching. When the sages taught people, it was not like this. People's dispositions range from high to low, their [self-cultivation] work may be raw or ripe, their learning may be shallow or deep. One should not as a general rule tell them of this [concept of innate knowledge]. This is why, when the sages taught people, what they said was sometimes based on people's defects, sometimes on their deficiencies, sometimes on what was one-sided in their learning. They never held fixed to one particular formulation.

"When it came to establishing fixed doctrines in order to instruct later generations, then they spoke of 'investigating things and extending knowledge,' 'accumulating broad learning of culture,' and 'restraining people with proper norms of conduct.' These generalizations can be used for establishing doctrines but not for [specific] application on the basis of how people are."

Lu Qian asked, "Desires are rooted in the mind. By what method can they be extirpated all at once?"

Master Lü said, "This is hard to explain. If you want to extirpate them all at once, you must work on it for a long time: only then will you succeed. Even a sage like Confucius, who at fifteen was intent on learning, had to reach thirty-five to be able to stand firm. Before this he inevitably had some minor vacillations from time to time.

"If you go wrong today in something you say or something you do, mentally check yourself and control it. You should not let yourself do this again. If you go wrong another day in something you say or do, again in your mind check yourself and control it like this. Even if no one else knows that you went wrong here,

23

you yourself know it. Control it and do not let it sprout again. This is the work of 'being careful in solitude.' After a long time, when this has ripened, then you will spontaneously be equipped with the true pattern whether moving or still, and human desires will melt away by themselves without your noticing it. If you expect to get rid of all the roots of sickness with a moment's effort, this is impossible."

Shao said, "In recent days, I have had a lot of business with people. I am afraid I may neglect my study."

Master Lü said, "In that case, you should study right in the midst of your business with people. People today think business is business and study is study: they view them as separated into two different things. What is necessary is that dealing with practical affairs *be* study and that study *be* dealing with practical affairs. Only then will you see the truth that mind and affairs are harmonized into one and that essence and function have the same source."

Wu You asked, "In their minds, many people want fame. What about this?"

Master Lü said, "There is nothing wrong with wanting fame. But I wonder, in your mind, what kind of fame do you want? If your mind thinks of the crops, then it is a reputation for nurturing the people. If it is contracts, then it is a reputation for educating the people. How can you make your fame everlasting? If you seek it in the things that will make your reputation so, then you will succeed, and this is good. If you just engage in vain longings for fame and are unwilling to set to work on [what it takes to win fame], then you will not have fame."

People all differ in where they lose their minds. Some lose their minds to wealth and profit. Some lose their minds to food and drink. Some lose their minds to fine clothing. Some lose their minds to luxurious houses. Some lose their minds to power and position. Since where people lose their minds differs, each person must go to where he has lost it to gather it back in. This is being truly human.

If a person can turn back and examine himself [to find the root of his problems], then he can travel freely in all directions, and it is all a smooth road. If a person is always intent on blaming others [for his problems], then wherever he steps will be thorny brambles.

When I teach you to study proper norms of behavior, this is like a dam for water. If you have no norms to hold back your body, then when your breast fills up with a mass of selfish intentions, they will flow out in all directions.

ZHAN RUOSHUI

Zhan Ruoshui (1463–1557) was from a family of wealthy landowners in Guangdong province. He was a disciple of Chen Baisha, a noted exponent of Zhu Xi's philosophy, who had studied with Wu Yubi. In 1517, Zhan built himself an opulent residence near Canton and opened a school there. He accepted students and prescribed for them a rigorous program of study, which included reading the classics, group study, and sitting meditation.

From 1505 to 1540 Zhan Ruoshui had a successful career as an official, reaching the top positions in the Bureaus of Rites, Military Affairs, and Personnel. Wherever his official duties took him, he established lecture halls in honor of Chen Baisha. In the course of his long life, he attracted followers all over the country.

Though by no means an innovative thinker, Zhan Ruoshui ranks with Wang Yangming as one of the most influential teachers of the time.

When the ancients discoursed upon learning, they never talked about stillness. Those who talked about stillness were always the

Zen people. The teachings of the Confucian school all want to seek true humanity in practical affairs.

Those who learn well are sure to unify movement and stillness in reverence.

When you work at learning, the mind does not run around outside: this is the means by which to seek lost mind.

The most crucial point is to handle things with reverence.

To nurture the mind you must use reverence. Making progress in learning is a matter of extending knowledge. Only if nurturing the mind and extending knowledge are both present is it proper learning.

Learning is no more than knowledge and action. They should not be separated, nor should they be confused together. Wherever you are, if you recognize Heaven's true pattern and nurture it, then knowledge and action will advance side by side.

What is called "being disjointed" has two meanings. To pursue the outer and forget the inner is not the only meaning of being disjointed. Being disjointed can also mean to affirm the inner and reject the outer. To go too far is as [wrong as] not going far enough. To avoid this one must have one source for essence and function and no gap between the subtle and the manifest: everything must be pervaded by oneness.

In learning, firmly establishing your will is the first priority, and knowing the basis is essential.

When you know the basis, you establish your will. When you have established your will firmly, then your mind does not get lost. When your mind does not get lost, then your true nature can be recovered. When your true nature is recovered, your lot will be settled, and then when vexations and anger come they will not entangle your mind's true nature.

In the learning of the sages, there is no opposition between nurturing the mind when in stillness and investigating things when in motion. This is a single work of self-cultivation.

It is just Heaven's true pattern. This is the principle focus that the thousand sages all share. Throughout our lives, it is just this great matter: there is nothing else.

When we establish our will, it is our will for this. When we do the work of recognizing this, it is just in order to find this. When we cut away and dissolve conditioned mind, it is in order to do away with what harms this. It is just a single good mind: fundamentally Heaven's true pattern is complete and perfect. It does not have to be sought outside.

Heaven's true pattern: each and every person inherently possesses it. It is not an external adornment. It is not preserved [only in a great sage like] Yao or destroyed by [an archvillain like] Jie. Therefore, all people can become [sages like] Yao and Shun by means of it. The mind of the man in the street is identical to the mind of Yao and Shun: it is all one mind, there is no other. Beginning students and the sages have this mind in common, share alike in this single true pattern of Heaven.

Someone expressed the worry that Heaven's true pattern is hard to see.

[Master Zhan's disciple] Chong replied: "You must seek it in your mind. Heaven's true pattern has no form: it is just this empty luminous awareness spread out before you."

Master Zhan said: "When you are correct in your mind, Heaven's true pattern will spontaneously appear. It is hard for you to see because your work on your mind is not yet correct."

In learning, it is important to melt away conditioned mind. The mind's conditioned habits are not inherent in it. They are only present due to particular configurations of circumstances: they are received as external qualities.

For example, the people of the arid northwest border region are fierce, the people of the populous wealthy central region are tricky. [This shows] the relationship of the mind's habits to climatic conditions. People who live in rich households are crass and avaricious, people who live in luxury are extravagant and wasteful. [This shows] the relationship of the mind's habits to how people live and are brought up. Thus [Confucius said], "By nature we are close [to the Tao]. Because of our habits, we are far from it."

Melting away [conditioned habits] is so called [by analogy with] refining gold. Gold can be mixed with lead, with copper, and with other impurities. These cannot be gotten rid of unless the gold is refined. Thus, gold must be smelted down a hundred times before it is pure. The mind must be refined a hundred times before it is illuminated.

The learning of the sages has always been the learning of mind. What we call mind does not mean something within us, something in our inner hearts, as opposed to external things. There is nothing that is not mind. When Yao and Shun held to the Mean, this does not mean only in regard to things: it means that mind and things were joined as one.

Do all of you realize that being loyal and trustworthy is the consummation of the Path of the sages? When those engaged in learning just boast of it to people and have no real virtue, it is because they are not loyal and trustworthy. Thus, the main thing is to be loyal and trustworthy. Being loyal and trustworthy is the means to advance in virtue, until you comprehend Heaven's virtue above and reach the Path of perfect integrity.

HONG YUAN

Hong Yuan won the highest degree in 1532 and had a career as a district administrator before retiring into private life to work as a scholar and teacher. He had studied with Zhan Ruoshui and opposed the philosophy of Wang Yangming.

If a morally developed person dispenses with human fellow-feeling, how can he be worthy of the name?

Begin thinking from the standpoint of human desires, and you are walking in danger. Begin thinking from the standpoint of Heaven's true pattern, and you are walking in safety.

When the will is unified, then it moves the vital energy. Once the vital energy moves, then the mind moves. When Mencius spoke of nurturing the vital energy, he meant that the will should be perfected and that vital energy should be united with the will. Thus he said, "Hold to will, and do not do violence to the vital energy." When the vital energy is at peace, the mind is at peace. Mind and will are both where the vital energy gathers.

Will and vital energy are similar. Where the will goes, the vital energy follows.

When Confucius and Mencius spoke of being reverent, of gathering together virtues, of being pure and unified and engaging in broad learning and being bound by proper norms, this was all a single holistic work of self-cultivation. They did not mean attending to things situation by situation and occasion by occasion.

At dawn, before we come in contact with things, there is nothing that can be liked or disliked. Why did Confucius say the Tao is close to people? It was because when the vital energy is pure and clear, there are no likes or dislikes: then the Tao is close.

Following true nature is called the Tao. If we proceed by following our true nature, then it goes without saying that we will be stable. To be stable means to follow true nature.

If mind does not enter into the fine subtleties, then it is still covered over by the coarseness of infatuation with sound and form, concern with profit and fame, and conditioned opinions.

If you stop conceit, then even though you are not good at learning, there will still be a time when learning can be used. It is like cutting off a chronic disease: once it is cut off, the primal energy returns by itself.

People live within a great cycle. Good fortune, ill fortune, repentance, stinginess [follow each other] without a stop. The sages look upon the true pattern of the Tao in accordance with this: they too never stop. If there is some obstruction in their conduct, they are sure to think of a means by which to get through it. Their wisdom grows clearer and clearer.

If we want to throw open the road ahead, we must first push down the wall that's facing us. What wall is this? The wall is in our minds. If our minds are not covered over, then all affairs under Heaven are within the purview of our investigation of things and our extension of knowledge. Thus, when things have been investigated and our intent has been made genuine, then our minds are broad and our bodies are at ease.

Zou Shouyi once said, "The ancients valued time highly. Even fifteen minutes was worth a thousand gold pieces." So how many gold pieces is a year's time worth? Since we did not sell it to

30

anyone else, and we did not use it ourselves, I wonder where we put it? In fact we have wasted it and kept nothing. What a pity!

We should always make our minds have riches to spare, and always make our actions relaxed, and follow our true nature. Then we will naturally be generous and broad-minded and expansive and free. When changing circumstances come, we will be able to perceive clearly what is right and what is wrong. We should not exhaust our minds and our strength, so that both become harried and constricted and cannot spread out.

If you are taken over by affairs, your actions will be many, but your mind will be narrow.

If those engaged in learning lack the will to work for the whole nation, then they lack the will to act on their own behalf.

When true knowledge flows, then knowledge and action advance side by side.

The fault of people is that each follows his own partisan faction. Partisanship is born from biases.

The anger of the sages comes from true human fellow-feeling. Our anger comes from our own personal ideas.

FENG CONGWU

Feng Congwu (1556–1627?) won the highest degree in 1589 and became a Hanlin Academy member. He entered the Censorate and narrowly escaped flogging for his criticism of the emperor's drinking and sexual excesses. In 1596 he and fourteen other censors were cashiered and stripped of their official rank. Feng

Congwu spent the next twenty-five years in his home area teaching at an academy he had established. He criticized the Wang Yangming school for being under Buddhist influences and wrote lengthy refutations of Buddhism.

We get life from the true pattern of Heaven and Earth. This is what is called our true nature with its principles of righteousness. Our vital energy and physical bodies are the means by which we bear this true pattern. How could we abandon our vital energy and physical bodies and look somewhere else for the principles of righteousness? Our true nature is actually one single thing. When we speak of principles of righteousness, the true pattern of moral duty, this includes our vital energy and our physical bodies.

The human mind possesses this true pattern from the first. Thus, if we see a baby about to fall into a well, we all feel alarmed and we all empathize with the situation. At such a time, there is certainly no room for the slightest thought of being merciless or cruel, nor are we motivated [to try to save the baby] by any thought of winning praise.

Investigating things means learning: it is wrong to talk of mysteries and emptiness.

The words "satisfied with oneself" have a deep meaning. When a petty person feels a sense of aversion upon seeing a morally developed person, it is precisely because the petty person feels dissatisfied with himself. How can his mind and body be content? Thus it is said, "If there is something in your conduct that does not satisfy your mind, you are hungry."

When a morally developed person is careful about his conduct even when alone [with no one to see how he acts], it is because he finds a sense of satisfaction in his own mind. With self-satisfaction, then one's intent become genuine. The expansive wave of vital energy [described by Mencius] fills Heaven and Earth.

Worldly Wisdom

How does a little child know to love? When he grows up a bit, how does he know how to be reverent? This must be because the ability to know love and reverence is already there in him. This is something with which Heaven has already endowed him when his parents first give birth to him. If you recognize this, then you recognize the true nature with which Heaven has endowed us.

If you do no evil to people, in the end, you have just become a pretender to virtue. Only when you have no evil intent are you a truly moral person.

The empty awareness of the human mind cannot be deceived in the least about what is right and what is wrong, what is permissible and what is not. Inherent in this mind is a measuring scale for whatever has to do with when to act and when to stop. If we are willing to rely on this fundamental mind in our conduct, and satisfy this mind in all matters, this is gathering together virtue, this is reflecting back and finding ourselves to be upright. This is precisely the tradition that Mencius received via [Confucius's disciple] Zeng Zi.

Some people live long lives, some die young. These are commonplace events. But most people consider dying young a deviation and living a long life the norm.

Sometimes we are slandered, sometimes we are praised. These are commonplace events. But most people consider being slandered a deviation and being praised the norm.

Sometimes we succeed, sometimes we fail. These are commonplace events. But most people consider failure a deviation and success the norm.

It is the same with poverty and wealth, with glory and disgrace.

[In fact what people distinguish as] "the norm" and "the deviation" are equally likely. It is wrong to make this distinction. Because of this people live their whole lives striving and seeking: how much arrogance, how much envy! It all comes from considering good fortune the norm and ill fortune the deviation. If you can see through this, then you will recognize that all these things—long life and early death, slander and praise, success and failure, poverty and wealth, glory and disgrace—all are commonplace events in human life, and you will not divide them. This is [the Confucian virtue of] "cultivating your personal existence in order to await your fate."

Our mission as Confucians does not lie beyond bringing good order and just peace.

To consider a family in order when it is wealthy and the country at peace when it is rich and strong is the tyrant's concept of order and peace, not the true monarch's order and peace.

When we see the father compassionate and the children filial, the husband amiable and the wife compliant, this is what an orderly family looks like. Whether the family is poor or rich has nothing to do with it. If we extend this to a state, human fellow-feeling and a sense of deference to others must prevail before a state can be said to be in good order. If we extend this to the whole country, the whole country is at peace only when kin are treated as kin and elders are treated as elders.

It is not a matter of whether the country is rich or not or whether the army is strong or not. To consider riches and strength as order and peace: this is the barrier that has not been broken for a thousand years.

There is no room for the [unregenerate] human mind and the mind of the Tao to stand side by side. When it comes to the guiding principles and constant norms and the true pattern of human relations, if we can fulfill this path, then it is the mind of the Tao. If we cannot fulfill it, then it is the [unregenerate] human mind. If our emotions are expressed with proper proportion, then it is the mind of the Tao. If they are out of proportion, then it is the [unregenerate] human mind. If our seeing and hearing and words and actions accord with the proper norms of behavior, then it is the mind of the Tao. If not, it is the [unregenerate] human mind. It is very easy to tell them apart.

The whole essence of the Tao of learning lies in penetrating to the source and gaining power before the emotions come forth. Then when they do come forth, they will always be in proper proportion, and whatever we encounter around us we will spontaneously meet with the source. In whatever we do, we will spontaneously stop at the proper point.

The superior person considers going along with the true pattern to be following his true nature. The petty person considers indulging his desires as following his true nature.

WANG YANGMING

Wang Yangming (1471–1529) was one of the most influential thinkers in Chinese history. His philosophy substantially reshaped Confucianism in sixteenth- and early seventeenth-century China.

Wang Yangming was a brilliant scholar who took first place in the official examinations. He had an eventful career as an imperial official both in the provinces and in the central bureaucracy, and he was no stranger to the intrigues of contemporary politics. He was a highly successful leader both in civil administration and in military campaigns.

He was well acquainted with both Taoism and Zen Buddhism, and Confucians who opposed him pointed out the similarities of his teachings to Zen. Nevertheless, many Confucians turned to his teachings during the period of intense change that overtook Chinese society in the sixteenth and seventeenth centuries. Wang Yangming inspired several generations of teachers and thinkers who came to constitute the mainstream of Confucianism during this turbulent era.

From the preface to the *Chuanxilu:*

When Master Wang Yangming heard that some of his disciples were privately making records of his words, he told them: "When the sages instructed people, they were like doctors using medicine. They always formulated the prescription according to the disease. They made a careful diagnosis and adjusted the treatment accordingly. The essential point was to get rid of the disease. They never had any fixed doctrines. If they stuck rigidly to a single prescription, mostly they would have killed people.

"When I deal with all of you, I do no more than admonish each person and hone each person according to his biases and blind spots. All I can do is transform these. Thus, my words are already an excrescence. If you were then to hold onto them as set lessons, later on you would lead yourselves and others into error. This would be my fault: how could I make up for it later?"

The ultimate good is to have this mind pure in the ultimate reaches of Heaven's true pattern.

Sincere belief [in the teaching of the sages] is certainly right, but it is not as cogent as verifying the truth within yourself. If at present you have not found the truth in your mind, then how can you dogmatically follow what you have heard in the past, without seeking to find out if it is correct?

Does clearly understanding the Tao make you return to simplicity and honesty, as seen in the real substance of your deeds? Or does it mean only to make a lot of noise in the world with fair words?

The great chaos in the world is due to the triumph of empty words and the decline of genuine practice.

The sages just wanted to cut away complicated verbiage. Later Confucians just wanted to add to it.

The laws of [the sage kings] Wen and Wu were identical to the Tao of [the even earlier sage kings] Yao and Shun, but they implemented their rule according to the times, and their institutions and policies were already different. It would not have been fitting to try to carry out the deeds of an earlier era in their own time.

To want to preserve Heaven's true pattern every moment: this is being intent [on the Tao]. If you are capable of not forgetting this, then after a long time it will spontaneously become solidified in your mind. This is what the Taoists call "forming the embryo of sagehood."

This is something that must be worked on every day. If you feel yourself getting confused, then sit quietly. If you feel yourself getting lazy, study books. In this too, the medicine must fit the disease.

When the sages wrote books, it was to describe reality and transmit the spirit. All they could do was sketch the general outline, so that people could follow this and seek the reality. There are indeed aspects of their spirit and energy, their words and laughter and actions, that could not be transmitted.

When those in later generations compose their works, they take what the sages have pictured and try to imitate it and copy it. They make their own false analyses and additions, in order to show off their cleverness. They have lost the reality more and more.

When one of his followers became unbearably sad upon receiving the news that his son was gravely ill, Master Wang said: "This is precisely the time you should work on yourself. If you let yourself go now, then what is the use of the learning you acquired while you were at ease? People must polish and refine themselves at such times. A father's love for his son is naturally an intense emotion, but in Heaven's true pattern there is also a way to have balance and harmony in this. If you go too far, it is selfishness."

We must do what is right according to the situation. It is impossible to determine a definite rule in advance. Latter-day

Confucians want to establish a general formula. This is [what Mencius criticized as] clinging to one [formula].

If people do not work at it, they always think they already know. When they study, they just follow [what they think they know] and practice that. They do not realize that selfish desires are born every day. It is like the dust on the ground: if it is not swept away each day, then another layer is added.

If you apply genuine effort, then you will see that the Tao is endless and infinite. The farther you delve into it, the deeper it is. You must purify yourself completely until there is nothing you do not penetrate.

People must have the intention to help themselves: only then will they be able to control themselves. Only when they can control themselves can they perfect themselves.

What the sages look like belongs to the sages. Where can we go to recognize it? If we do not go to our own innate knowledge to get genuine direct recognition, it is like trying to weigh something with a scale that has no calibration marks. This is truly what is called "taking a petty person's belly to measure a profound person's heart." [If we do this] how will we be able to recognize what the sages look like? Our own innate knowledge is the same as that of the sages. If we can clearly recognize our own innate knowledge, then what the sages look like is not in the sages, but in us.

"Without thinking of good or evil, recognize your original face." The Buddhists set this forth as an expedient for those who have not yet recognized their original face. The original face is equivalent to what we in the school of the Confucian sages call innate moral knowledge.

True nature is one. Human fellow-feeling, a sense of moral duty, proper norms of behavior, wisdom: these are the true nature of true nature. Intelligence and understanding are the substance of true nature. Joy, anger, grief, happiness: these are the emotions of true nature. Selfish desires, alien energies: these are what cover over true nature.

Innate moral knowledge *is* the Tao. Innate moral knowledge is in the human mind: it is this way not only in the sages, but also in ordinary people. If you are not dragged off or covered by material desires, if you just follow the function and flow of innate moral knowledge, then nothing is not the Tao.

Learning is just learning how to follow this innate moral knowledge, that's all.

Every person has a sage within his breast. It is just that people do not fully believe in this sage and bury it away.

Innate moral knowledge is present in everyone: no matter how you are, you cannot obliterate it. Even a robber knows he should not rob. If you call him a robber, he will look ashamed.

If people can recognize innate moral knowledge, this vital secret, then no matter how many perverse ideas and false thoughts they have, once they become aware [of their innate moral knowledge] here [in the midst of perverse ideas and false thoughts], these all spontaneously dissolve away. This is really the spiritual elixir that can transmute iron into gold.

There was an administrator who had listened for a long time to Master Wang's lectures on learning and commented, "This learning is very good. It's just that my account books and legal briefs are many and complicated and difficult, and I have no opportunity to study."

When Wang Yangming heard this, he said, "When have I ever told you to leave your account books and legal briefs behind and go engage in learning in a void? Since you have official business to attend to, you should engage in learning right in the midst of this official business. This would be genuine 'investigation of things.' "

When we Confucians nurture the mind, we never depart from things and events. We just follow their natural laws given by Heaven: this is our work.

When we eat, it is to nourish our bodies. After we have eaten, we must digest. If the food were to just pile up in our bellies, we would get constipated.

Students in these later generations accumulate a lot of information, but it just gets stuck inside them. This is a case of indigestion.

Someone asked, "How is it that even a great sage like Confucius did not avoid slander?"

Wang Yangming said, "Slander comes from outside. How can even a sage avoid it? People should just consider their own self-cultivation as the important thing. If someone is genuinely a sage, then even if people all slander him, their words cannot touch him. How can floating clouds that cover the sun damage the sun's light?"

In our work of learning and self-cultivation, we may be able to get free of all our concerns for reputation and gain and get free of our desires, but if we still have some concern for birth and death hanging over us, then there still is not total fusion of the complete essence. Human beings carry a concern with birth and death with them from the root of being born into physical existence, and so it is hard to get rid of it. Only if we can see through this, and penetrate through it, will the complete essence of this mind flow without obstruction. This alone is the learning of complete realization of our true nature and knowledge of our destiny.

When Dong Luoshi returned from a walk outside, he saw Master Wang and said, "Today I saw something extraordinary."

Master Wang said, "What was so extraordinary?"

Dong Luoshi said, "I saw that the people who fill the streets are all sages."

Master Wang said, "This is something commonplace. How can you think it extraordinary?"

Several of Master Wang's disciples had returned from taking the official examinations, and they told him that as they lectured along the way, some people believed and some did not.

Master Wang said, "If you dragged a sage along to lecture to people, when the people saw the sage coming, they would all run in fright. How could the lecture proceed? You must act like an ordinary ignorant man or woman to be able to lecture to people."

The great disease in human life is arrogance. An arrogant child cannot be filial, an arrogant minister cannot be loyal, an arrogant father cannot be compassionate, an arrogant friend cannot be trustworthy.

All the good points of the ancient sages were just a matter of being free from egotism. If you can be free of egotism, then you can be humble. Humility is the basis of the myriad virtues. Arrogance is the chief of the many evils.

If your will for the Tao is earnest, this is surely a sincere intent. But to seek it hastily becomes selfishness instead. You must be clear about this. In your daily activities, what is there that is not the flow of the true pattern of Heaven? Just always preserve this mind and do not let it go astray, and then the true pattern of righteousness will ripen by itself.

The mind of the sages of itself has no room for the slightest obscuring factor. It does not need to be polished. As for the mind of ordinary people, it is like a mirror that is streaked with dirt. It must be vigorously polished clean. Only after the streaks are totally removed will the finer particles of dust [that remain] be seen. As soon as you wipe these away, they will be gone, and this naturally does not take a lot of effort. After you have reached this stage, you will recognize the essential body of true humanity.

When our minds deal with things and events purely according to the true pattern, with no admixture of human falsity, this is called goodness. It is not that there is something definite in things and events that we should seek. "Dealing with things properly is righteousness" means that our mind finds what is proper to it. Righteousness is not something external that we can follow and grasp.

If there is no attitude of gaining advantage in me, then [no matter what I do], whether I make money or farm or serve as a soldier or carry firewood or haul water, everywhere I go is genuine study, and everything is Heaven's true pattern.

If I still have the attitude of gaining advantage, then even if I spend my days speaking of the Tao and its virtues and true humanity and righteousness, this is all just the business of gaining advantage.

You must want this mind purely in accord with the true pattern of Heaven, without any of the selfishness of human desires. This is what must be accomplished to be a sage. If you want to do this, you will not be able to unless you guard against [selfish desires] before they sprout and control them as soon as they have sprouted. This is precisely [what is called] "being careful and cautious" in The Doctrine of the Mean and "extending knowledge and investigating things" in The Great Learning. There is no other accomplishment beyond this.

What a morally developed person calls happiness is not endless indulgence, giving free rein to one's own feelings and wishes.

Rather, [to such a person happiness] means not having the mind's essence entangled with desires, so that one can go anywhere and be satisfied.

As for the fundamental essence of the mind, it is identical to the true pattern of Heaven. The clear spiritual awareness of Heaven's true pattern is what is called innate knowledge. When a profound person is "careful and cautious," his only fear is that his clear spiritual awareness will somehow be dimmed and lost and flow into error and falsity and lose the correctness of its basic essence.

If the work of being "careful and cautious" is never interrupted, then Heaven's true pattern will always be preserved [in your mind], and the basic essence of clear spiritual awareness will not be lacking or covered over or be dragged off or disturbed. There will be no fear or worry, no craving or resentment, no stubborn selfish demands, no shame or embarrassment. You will be harmonious and suffused with light flowing through, filling everything. Your actions and demeanor will be completely in accord with the proper norms: you will follow your heart's desires without overstepping the bounds of propriety. This is what is called constant happiness. This happiness is born from always preserving Heaven's true pattern.

There is no such thing in the world as fully comprehending the true pattern without applying it in practice. Thus, knowing without acting cannot be considered learning, and knowing without acting cannot be considered fully comprehending the true pattern. Therefore it is evident that knowledge and action are joined as one and advance together: they should not be divided into two things.

The [role of] innate moral knowledge in events and changing situations is like [the function of] a compass and T-square and ruler [in marking out] squares and circles and lengths.

In general, in the work of learning, it is necessary to pay attention correctly to the vital starting point. If you focus your intent on the vital starting point, you will devote yourself to exercising innate knowledge. Then all you do to acquire learning will be the work of exercising innate knowledge. This is because in your daily activities, as you see things and hear things and interact with people in all kinds of ways, it will all be the functioning and flowing of innate knowledge. Apart from seeing and hearing and interacting with people, there would be no innate knowledge to be exercised.

Mind *is* the true pattern. This mind, without the covering of selfish desires, is identical to Heaven's true pattern. It is not necessary to add anything to it externally. When this mind that is purely Heaven's true pattern goes into action serving your father, then you are filial. When it goes into action serving the monarch, then you are loyal. When it goes into action forming friendships and bringing political order to the people, then you are trustworthy and have true human fellow-feeling. This is just the result of this mind getting rid of human desires and preserving the true pattern of Heaven.

[Knowledge and action] are split apart by selfish desires. The basic essence of knowledge and action is not this way. There is no such thing as knowledge that is not put into practice. To know without acting is in fact not to know. When the sages taught people to know and to put [knowledge] into practice, they wanted them to return to that basic essence.

[The sages] said that knowledge is the guiding idea for action and that action is the practical work of knowledge. Knowledge is the beginning of action, and action is the consummation of knowledge. If you understand [the sages], in fact what they said is that any knowledge already has action inherently within it, and any action already has knowledge inherently within it.

Ordinary people are [at first] unable to be free from selfish intentions. Therefore they must make the effort to extend their knowledge and investigate things, to overcome selfish biases and return to proper norms of behavior. Then innate moral knowledge will have no more obstacles and will flow out and fill everything. This is extending knowledge. When knowledge has been extended, intentions become sincere and true.

Mind is one. Before it is mixed with human falsity, it is called the mind of the Tao. When it is mixed with human falsity, it is called the human mind. When the human mind attains its correct state, it is identical to the mind of the Tao. When the mind of the Tao loses its correct state, it is identical to the human mind. Master Cheng Yi said that the human mind is human desire, and the mind of the Tao is Heaven's true pattern.

People must polish and refine themselves in the midst of practical affairs. Only then can they stand firm, only then can they be stable whether at rest or in motion.

Innate moral knowledge is your own personal standard. If you are conscious of it, then when something is right, you will immediately know it is right, and when something is wrong, you will immediately know it is wrong. Nothing will be able to deceive you. You must not play false with it. Be very genuine and true, and base your actions on it. Then you will keep what is good and get rid of what is evil. How secure you will be! This is the real accomplishment of extending knowledge.

When we extend knowledge, we do so to the extent of our capacity. If today my innate knowledge is like this, then according to what I know today, I extend it to the maximum. If tomorrow my innate knowledge has an awakening, then according to what I know tomorrow, I extend it to the maximum. To act like this is the work of purifying and unifying.

WANG JI

After 1521, when Wang Yangming returned to his hometown of Yuyao in Zhejiang province, Wang Ji (1498–1583) was among the first of his disciples. Wang Ji established the Tianzhen Academy in the metropolis of Hangzhou, dedicated to spreading Wang Yangming's teachings. He received the highest degree in 1532 and pursued an official career for ten years. His objections to factional favoritism aroused the antagonism of the top bureaucrat Xia Yan, so Wang Ji resigned from office in 1542.

Wang Ji spent the remaining forty years of his life traveling widely to teach. He was familiar with Taoism and Buddhism, and he saw them as in essence compatible with Confucian learning. Wang Ji is counted among the most influential followers of Wang Yangming, and several of his own disciples became prominent teachers and thinkers.

The means by which a sage is a sage is the lifeline of the spirit functioning whole within him. He does not seek acknowledgment from people. Thus he is always on the lookout for his own faults and does not content himself with falsity. Day by day he progresses toward the infinite.

A man who pretends to wisdom and virtue is intent on currying favor with the world. He takes care of the whole spirit only on the outside. Thus he considers himself correct but cannot enter into the Path of [the early sages] Yao and Shun.

Extending innate moral knowledge is just responding to things with an empty mind, to enable all people to live to the full their true nature. [In extending innate moral knowledge], you can be hard or you can be soft. As you come in contact with situations, you respond; when you meet a sharp edge, you part before it. You are like a clear mirror in empty space: beautiful and ugly are distinct by themselves. Only this is the sage's method to deal with

46

all things. As soon as there is intellectual trickery, and you try to impose [a fixed] shape [on innate knowledge], your own light is covered over.

All the worldly emotions and desires that we have as people are born from intent. Mind itself is fundamentally good, but when it moves to intent, there begin to be things that are not good.

If you can establish your basis in the primordial mind-essence, then the motion of intent will of itself be free of things that are not good. There will be no place for worldly emotions and desires. The work of extending knowledge will naturally be easy, and energy will be saved.

If you establish your basis at the temporal level of moving intent, you will not avoid the admixture of worldly emotions and desires, and the work of extending knowledge will feel even more complicated and difficult.

If the will you establish is not genuine, then your effort will inevitably be interrupted. You must understand thoroughly from the fundamental source. You must totally cut off all kinds of desires, all kinds of cravings and attachments, all kinds of special abilities, and all the habits and attitudes of ordinary mind. Make yourself completely clean.

When my late master [Wang Yangming] was teaching, [on one occasion] there was a man whose nature was alert and quick, but the master treated him indifferently and did not answer his repeated questions. There was another man who paid no attention to criticism and was detested by the others from his hometown. The master would talk to him tirelessly all day long. I was in doubt about this and asked the master [why he acted this way].

Yangming said, "Though the first man is indeed alert and quick by nature, he is unwilling to abandon his worldly sentiments and mental machinations. If I do not let him hear any teachings, a time will come when his shortcoming is revealed to him and he repents.

47

"If I were to let him hear my teachings, his opinions and interpretations would become even more numerous, his evasions would become even more clever, and what covers him would become even thicker. All his carefully synthesized knowledge and thoughts would become evil and would be impossible to reform.

"The other man is actually a man of great strength. For the moment he is unable to dissolve away his crazy ideas and stop them. Once he has repented, he will shift his strength to do good, and he will be able to accomplish everything.

"This is why I treated these two men differently."

My late master said of himself, "Before I lived among the barbarians, nine out of ten praised me. Before [my appointment to the prestigious] Honglu Academy, five out of ten praised me, and five out of ten criticized me. After Honglu, nine out of ten criticized me. The more true my learning became, the more people saw it as wrong. Those who had previously acclaimed my ideas concealed this and dissimulated, so people could not see."

Extending innate knowledge begins from the living potential. Only this is the learning of seeing true nature.

How can you control idle miscellaneous thoughts? You must be careful and wary with the Tao which you neither see nor hear. If you function from your true potential, you will be spontaneously free of this sickness.

Joy is the basic essence of mind. Mind is basically leaping with life, basically free and untrammeled, basically without obstructions and bonds. [The sage kings of antiquity] Yao and Shun and Wen and Wu were so careful and cautious and respectful and consistently strong because they preserved this essence and did not lose it. This potential, leaping with life and utterly free, cannot be added to.

Innate moral knowledge is the natural, luminously aware potential. It is constantly rolling out from the natural potential, transforming and teaching, speaking and acting, spontaneously manifesting the rules of nature. You must not block it. You must not search for it. How could it ever be taken charge of or not taken charge of?

Knowledge is the essence of mind. All people have what is called the mind of right and wrong. Right and wrong are fundamentally clear: it is not necessary to borrow them. [The mind of right and wrong] responds according to how it is affected and is always spontaneous.

The sagely learning centers on being able to trust yourself. When you affirm what is right and reject what is wrong, this does not come from outside. Thus, if you are sure something is right, you should do it. Even if it is out of sight of the world and is not seen as right, you have no worries. If you are sure something is wrong, you must definitely not do it. Even if you could gain the world by doing one unrighteous thing or killing one innocent person, you would not do it. Only if you act like this will you not be deceiving yourself. Only this can be called the Tao of the True King. How simple and direct!

The students in later generations have not been able to trust themselves. They have inevitably come to depend on outside things and have been moved by glory and disgrace. Thus they consider blame and praise as [the criteria for] right and wrong and are careful about what can benefit and what can harm [their reputations]. Thus they consider success and failure [the criteria for] right and wrong and mix together false borrowings and devious arrangements, so things appear more and more complex and difficult. In the end, all they can achieve are the maneuvers of tyrants, and the simple learning of the sages can no longer be seen.

Innate knowledge is the pure spiritual awareness of creation and transformation. As human beings, we must take creation and transformation as our study. From nonbeing, creation manifests being. From being, transformation returns to nonbeing. Our pure awareness gives birth to heaven, earth, and the myriad things, and heaven, earth, and the myriad beings in turn go back to nonbeing. There is no time when creation and transformation are not operating: they never stop or pause.

The basic essence of innate knowledge is originally without movement or stillness, and it is originally transformation and circulation. This is the key starting point for learning. If you do not see the basic essence of innate knowledge, then you will just be picking and choosing between movement and stillness, grasping one and rejecting the other. Then it will either be false movement or getting attached to stillness. In both cases you will fail to get nourishment.

The basic essence that is here right now is like the path of birds in flight through the sky, like the reflections of the moon in a river. It seems to be there, and it seems not to be there. It seems to sink down, and it seems to float up. If you try to think about it, you go against it. If you go toward it, you are turning your back on it even more. The spirit potential responds wondrously while fundamentally empty in its very essence: where can you recognize it? If you attain awakening at this, only then is it the true face in the midst of formlessness. Without exerting the slightest effort, it is where you exert the greatest effort.

The bit of empty illumination that is innate knowledge is the potential to be a sage. If you preserve this bit of empty illumination at all times and do not let it be fettered and destroyed in your daily activities, this is extending innate knowledge.

Anger does not mean only angry outbursts. Any jealousy or narrow-mindedness or intolerance or feelings of irritation and unwillingness to let little things go: all of this is anger. Desire does not mean only lust. Any infatuation with entangling objects, so that the mind turns over and over; any craving and unwillingness to give things up: all of this is desire.

The work of warning against anger and preventing desire can be hard or easy. You can work at the level of things and events, at the level of thoughts, or at the level of mind. At the level of things and events, you block anger and desire after they have already occurred. At the level of thoughts, you curb them as they are about to occur. At the level of mind, you prevent them before they occur. Warning the mind against anger and blocking the mind's desires: this alone is the fundamental work, the easy work. If you try to curb anger and desire at the level of things and events or the level of thoughts, even if you do your utmost to wipe them away, you will never be completely clear of them.

The way vulgar people consider themselves good and the behavior of the truly good are clearly two different paths. The truly good have confidence in fundamental mind: they affirm what is right and reject what is wrong and do not change to follow people at all. When vulgar people consider themselves good, they are putting on a facade of virtue. They are unable to trust in their own [innate moral knowledge], and they inevitably accept what people praise as good and what people censure as bad.

Innate moral knowledge is not [attained by] learning or thought. When we study and learn all day long, it is just to recover its essence, which is not learned. When we think all day long, it is just to recover its essence, which is not [attained by] thought.

The true work has no work: [innate moral knowledge] cannot be added to. The work [of self-cultivation] is just seeking day by day to diminish [one's anger and desires]: it is not seeking to increase anything. When [anger and desires] have been reduced to the point of total elimination, then you are a sage.

The learning and techniques of later generations are just tricks to add things. Therefore, though they work hard all day, they further increase their sickness. If you can actually have a moment of wakefulness, then you will coolly, spontaneously become good. To exhaust the functioning [of innate knowledge] is ultimately impossible. This is the final word.

In the world there is just knowledge. Knowledge that is not put into action is not worth calling knowledge.

Because later Confucians had separated them into two, my late master [Wang Yangming] had no choice but to speak of them being joined as one.

The human mind is empty and illuminated: its essence is profoundly clear. Originally it is leaping with life: how could it be held fast? Just cultivate it according to the occasion. It undergoes transformation and circulation, sometimes favorable, sometimes adverse, sometimes going in one direction, sometimes in another: follow whatever it does, and return to its live essence, without being obstructed by objects. This is called preserving [mind].

With this matter, it is not that you speak of it and then stop. You must work on it all the time. You always have faults you should correct. Only when you wipe away the force of habit and reach the light is it the glorious learning. In this learning there is no small or large, no inside or outside. Your speech and your conduct are the means by which you solidify the Tao.

If you are a person who sees true nature, then true nature flows everywhere, filling up everything equally wherever you are: the natural potential is always alive, without any excess or deficit, and there are naturally no contrived arrangements. Only this is being sure of yourself.

The learning of the sages for a thousand ages is just recognized in a moment of spiritual illumination.

Immediately preserve this moment of spiritual illumination: this is learning.

To use this to make contact with people, to develop them, to influence them, and to communicate with them: this is teaching.

Not to dim this moment of spiritual illumination whatever you are doing: this is called investigating things.

Not to deceive this moment of spiritual illumination: this is called making your intent genuine and sincere.

A moment of emptiness, without the least bit of inherent selfishness: this is called keeping the mind correct. This is the simple direct root source.

In our master Yangming's school, there are three kinds of teaching on enlightenment. To get it by knowing and understanding is called enlightenment by understanding. This does not go beyond verbal explanations. To get it in stillness is called enlightenment by witnessing. This is still relative to objects. To get it from refining oneself amidst human affairs, so that words and objects are forgotten, and wherever you touch you meet the source, so that the more you are shaken, the more solid your stillness: only this is total penetrating enlightenment.

Innate moral knowledge is in people: it is in the daily activities of the common folk the same as in the accomplishments of the sages. Originally it has no room for people to add anything or take away anything for it to be complete.

The means by which people are people is nothing but spirit and vital energy. Spirit is the ruler of the vital energy. Vital energy is the flow of the spirit. Spirit is nature. Vital energy is life. Innate knowledge is the secret of spirit and vital energy, the key to nature and life. When innate knowledge is exercised, the spirit and physical energy communicate, and nature and life are whole. The working of this is not apart from the subtlety of a single moment of thought.

Investigating things, categorizing things, is the real ground to set to work in exercising knowledge. The categories used in the investigation are Heaven's natural principles, which innate knowledge inherently possesses: they are also what are called natural categories.

Just when myriad desires are boiling up, if you are willing to return to a moment of innate moral knowledge, what is truly right and wrong in them will always be clearly obvious. This is where Heaven's command cannot be extinguished, and the human mind cannot be obscured. For a thousand ages this has been the true and correct path for entering into sagehood.

If you say, "I will just gather myself in here and hold tight [to innate knowledge], so I have a key link that I can hold onto," and think that this is the real substance of exercising innate knowledge, you inevitably fall into a dualistic view of inner and outer. As soon as you are holding onto something, it always becomes forced control. This forced control is itself the cause for letting go and losing it [later].

Tell me, are there any attachments in a child's spirit or not? When an eagle flies, or a fish swims, is there any forced control? If you grasp something with your hand, there is bound to be a time when you let go. If you do not grasp it, it is secure by itself. This is forgetting the hand. This is just forgetting without anything to forget. Therefore, [mind] is preserved without having to be preserved. You should enlighten yourself to this.

QIAN DEHONG

Qian Dehong (1495–1574) was from Yuyao, Wang Yangming's hometown, and became his disciple when Yangming returned there in 1521. As people flocked there to study, Yangming put Wang Ji and Qian Dehong in charge of instructing newcomers. After Yangming died in 1529, Qian helped collect his sayings.

Qian Dehong won the highest degree in 1532 and became an official, first at the National Academy and then with the Bureau of Punishments. After he proposed that one of the imperial favorites should be punished for his misdeeds, Qian was imprisoned for two years. He retired from official life and for thirty years devoted himself to teaching, traveling all over South China.

Though the points they emphasized in Wang Yangming's philosophy differed, Qian Dehong and Wang Ji remained lifelong friends.

The sense of caution and diffidence is innate moral knowledge. To feel that you have a lot of this caution and diffidence is the birth of self-cultivation work. After a long time, this fundamental work can be forgotten: it is accomplished without thinking and hits the mark without effort. This is complete ripeness.

Thought is the life of the human mind. It cannot be stopped for a single moment. Just let this mind have a ruler that is ever firm, and what thought sends out will spontaneously have order and pattern. The process of natural creation and transformation is the ruler that is ever firm: that is why the four seasons and the sun and moon go back and forth without becoming disordered.

This mind, since time without beginning, is originally motionless. Though we may think thousands of thoughts, it is just that the workings of natural potential are spontaneously so. Though we may feel myriad influences and make myriad responses, from the beginning the fundamental essence has always been still.

It is just because we humans have our own knowledge and consciousness that what we strive for and what we desire—our abilities and perceptions and all our intentions—work surely to solidify our individual selves. We make for ourselves knowledge and views, we make for ourselves instabilities and vexations, and we lose the fundamental essence that is perfect and good, so we never get to stop. We must take such mental habits and totally abandon them. Only then will we be sure that fundamental inherent nature is actually like this.

In the midst of multiplicity and confusion, the sages point out the unmoving true essence. This is innate knowledge. This is knowing. Though they are subjected to a chaos of myriad influences, they are not confused about right and wrong. Though many desires press in on them, they embody purity and illumination. Perfectly adaptive, with no location; perfectly spiritual, with no traces: this is the essence of innate knowledge.

In the midst of the great void, [the true essence] has everything. But it does not abide in any one thing, because if it did, it would be obstructed by the great void. It is never without the influences and responses of the human mind, but it never dwells on them, because if it did, it would be blocked by empty awareness.

Therefore, as soon as anger and delight and fear and worry appear in the mind, the mind does not attain its correct state. Thus the work of keeping mind correct is not a matter of seeking anywhere else: it just lies in making the intent genuine. [The mind's] essence must be aligned with the illumination of the fundamental essence shining through, so it comes to rest in the ultimate good.

Just seek not to go against innate moral knowledge, then you will naturally penetrate through human sentiments. If you only seek not to go against human sentiments, then you will follow along with other people and forget yourself.

Someone asked, "Why can't I influence other people?"

Master Qian said, "As soon as you speak of influencing other people, this is already not right. The sages just made themselves correct, and others spontaneously corrected themselves. For example, when the sun is uncovered, its light spontaneously can shine on things. It does not make a special effort to go looking for things to shine on."

To get rid of evil, we must get to the bottom of its roots. When doing good we do not dwell on possessing it. This is the rule for investigating things. But it is not the ultimate learning where the basic essence stops at perfect goodness.

If we let the mechanism of good and evil go on endlessly, with each being born and being obliterated in turn, then this is hiding the root and not liking it when sprouts grow, this is muddying the source and thinking it will be clear downstream. In doing this, we take the knowledge of good and evil as the ultimate in knowledge, and we do not recognize that the essence of innate moral knowledge is fundamentally without good and evil; we think that contrived action to have good and get rid of evil is an accomplishment, and we do not realize that the ultimate basic essence works its accomplishments at the level of uncontrived reality, and this is true accomplishment.

Correct mindfulness is without thought. The mindfulness of correct mindfulness in fundamental essence is forever still. As soon as there is involvement with selfish and misguided thoughts, then we waver back and forth and fall into confusion.

If we penetrate through to this mind and are thoroughly free from desires, then even if we are dealing with all kinds of duties all day long, how can the slightest thing be added to the basic essence? After business is over and we stop, it totally passes without a trace: how can the slightest thing be taken away from the basic essence?

Spiritual penetration, wondrous enlightenment, is not apart from human relations and things and events. It is found in the true essence of humanity.

When it comes to this awakening of the mind, contemporary scholars say that the path to it is a rare spiritual secret, a covert potential, a hidden opening. They make people feel uncertain and unclear about it, make them feel that there is no place to enter. Surely, this is not the awakening of our true nature.

Once we hear of innate knowledge, we accept its influence. Without pondering or investigating very deeply, we use it to finally penetrate through to the true essence. Thus we do indeed attain the awakening of the mind.

Innate knowledge is vast and great and lofty and clear. Originally it has no false thoughts that can be removed. As soon as there are false thoughts to be removed, we have already lost the vast and great and lofty and clear essence. Right now just wake up the fundamental essence, and the many falsities will dissolve away by themselves.

The basic essence of mind is pure and unadulterated. It is perfectly good. Innate moral knowledge is the application of this perfect goodness to investigation. Innate knowledge is perfectly good.

Mind has no essence apart from knowing: without knowing there would be no mind. Knowing has no essence except being influenced by and responding to right and wrong: without right and wrong there would be no knowing.

Intent refers to being influenced and responding. Things are what influence [us] and are responded to. Knowing is the standard that rules the right and wrong of things and events. Intent may move or keep still, but the essence of this knowing is not illuminated or darkened by the movement or stillness of intent. Things may come or go, but the essence of this knowing is not present or absent according to the coming or going of things. The essence of our true nature flows on spontaneously without stopping.

Do not look for [innate knowledge] in the mind that has already gone astray. Look for it in the mind before it has gone astray. The essence of mind is our true nature. We cannot depart from our true nature. So how can mind get lost and go astray? When we say we have lost it, it means it is frantically pursuing things.

Innate moral knowledge and the natural true pattern are originally not two separate ideas. With reference to the mind's spiritual empty shining awareness, we call it knowledge. With reference to the mind's structured pattern, we call it true pattern. The spiritual empty shining awareness is as it is spontaneously, without having to be learned or thought about, so we call it innate. The structured pattern is as it is spontaneously, without having to be learned or thought about, so we call it natural.

When we speak of spiritual empty shining awareness, what we mean by shining awareness is [awareness of] the structured pattern. If the pattern did not appear in the spiritual empty shining awareness, then surely there would be no way by which it could act as innate moral knowledge. And if we had to search again for what we call the pattern in the midst of the spiritual empty shining awareness, then it surely would not be what we have called the natural pattern.

Human life is influenced by worldly sentiments. It is like a fish swimming in water: wherever it goes it is blocked, and there is no gap [to escape through].

The waves indeed arise in our own minds. If this mind is not dragged around or tied down by anything, then even if we are in contact with human sentiments and the vicissitudes of events every day, the true thusness [of our minds] will be independent, and we will respond to [sentiments and events] without getting stuck. Then there will be no more waves that can move us. This is what is called "stable when moving and stable when still."

If you do not avoid having this mind preoccupied with worldly sentiments, then even if you sit impassive in an empty studio and do not reveal any loose ends, still a hundred thoughts come to make you boil up, and you have no escape.

Students these days feel pained and upset as soon as they encounter things and events and immediately start longing for someplace quiet. But when they get to a quiet place, the vexation is still within them as before. This is precisely because they do not consider that movement and motionlessness are just in their own minds, not in things.

The work of making selections, extending knowledge, and investigating things must be recognized in things and events, so that fundamental mind can be seen there. When mind and events are not two, and inner and outer are both forgotten, then without getting away from things and events, you have some learning worth talking about.

WANG GEN

Wang Gen (1483–1541) came from a humble background, but he was to become perhaps the most charismatic of Wang Yangming's disciples. He had already formed his own philosophy when he first heard of Wang Yangming's ideas and was struck by their similarity to his own. He traveled to meet Yangming when he was governor of Jiangxi province and became his disciple. Wang Gen was an inspiring teacher and had students in all walks of life, down to the humblest artisans. The following are some incidents from his life story as recorded in *Ming Ru Xue-an*.

When he was seven he became a student at the village school. Because [the family] was poor, he could not complete his studies. He accompanied his father, who was a trader in Shandong. He always carried with him *The Classic of Filial Piety,* the *Analects,* and *The Great Learning,* and when he met [learned] people, he would question them about difficult passages.

His father was subject to corvée service [unpaid labor for the government]. The weather was cold, and his father had to wash in cold water. When Wang Gen saw this, he cried out in anguish: "How can I be a son and let my father do this and still be a man?" From then on, whenever there was any work [assigned to his father], Wang Gen took his place.

Though Wang Gen was unable to devote all his effort to his studies, nevertheless he pursued his studies in silence. He used the classics to attest to his awakening and used his awakening to explicate the classics. As the years went by, no one could fathom him.

Wang Gen noted this: "In 1511 I spent three and a half months 'abiding in true humanity.' From then on, whether walking or standing or speaking or silent, I was always in a state of awakening."

At this time, Wang Yangming was Pacification Commissioner in Jiangxi. He lectured on the study of innate moral knowledge, and scholars from the region all flocked to him and became his faithful followers. Because Wang Gen lived in a remote locale, he had not heard of Wang Yangming. There was a man from Ji-an named Huang Wengang who was passing through Taizhou and heard Wang Gen's discourses. He told him, "This is just like Wang Yangming's theory." Wang Gen was pleased and said, "So there is such a one!" . . .

That very day Wang Gen set off [to see Wang Yangming]. He went in to meet him wearing his archaic costume. He went as far as the threshold, held up his *hu* [the hand-plaque held by officials in ancient times when they were received at an imperial audience], and stood there. Wang Yangming came out to greet him.

As soon as Wang Gen entered [the hall], he sat in the place of honor. After he had discussed difficult points with Wang Yangming for a long while, he felt somewhat abashed and moved his seat to the side. After their talk was over, Wang Gen sighed and said, "I do not match him in simplicity and directness." He prostrated himself and declared himself to be Wang Yangming's disciple.

Wang Gen withdrew to ponder what he had heard. After a time, [he realized] that there were things he did not agree with. He felt regret and said, "I have been too casual." The next day he went back to see Wang Yangming and expressed his regrets. Wang Yangming said, "Excellent! You do not believe too easily." Wang Gen again sat in the place of honor. Only after a long discussion of difficult points was Wang Gen fully convinced. So he became a disciple as he had before.

Wang Yangming told his companions: "Before, when I captured [the rebel prince] Chen Hao I was totally unmoved. But today I have been moved by this man."

When Wang Yangming returned to [his hometown in] Zhejiang, Wang Gen followed him. Many of those who came to study received instructions from Wang Gen. After a time Wang Gen sighed to himself and said, "For a thousand years real learning has been cut off, but now Heaven has raised up my teacher [Wang Yangming]. How can I allow there to be any place in the country where they have not heard of him?"

At this time, there was a storm of slanderous criticism of Wang Yangming's theories. Wang Gen [who had gone to the capital to proselytize] did not dress or speak or act the same as other people, and the people in the capital looked upon him as a strange apparition. Wang Yangming's other followers in the capital urged Wang Gen to return home, and Yangming himself sent a letter admonishing him.

When Wang Gen first returned to Kuaiji, Yangming thought his attitude was too lofty and his behavior too unusual and censured him severely. Three days Wang Gen came to see him, but Yangming would not meet with him. When Yangming came out the gate to see off a visitor, Wang Gen was kneeling by the side of the path and said to him, "I have realized my error." But Yangming went back inside without looking at him. Wang Gen followed him into the courtyard and cried out, "Confucius was not this severe!" Only then did Yangming greet him and bid him arise.

Wang Gen returned to his home area [Taizhou], opened his gate, and accepted disciples. People came from far and near. When followers of Wang Yangming held lecture meetings, they were sure to invite Wang Gen to preside.

Among the disciples of Wang Yangming, Wang Ji was foremost in eloquence, but [when he lectured] some would believe him and some would not. It was Wang Gen who could bring insight and awakening to the most people in the blink of an eye.

Worldly Wisdom

Some samples of Wang Gen's teachings:

Being able to understand one's personal existence is the basis for the whole world. When you can do this, then the myriad things in Heaven and Earth will depend on you yourself, and you will not depend on them.

When essence and functioning are not at one, this is where the work [of self-cultivation] is born.

The Tao of the sages is no different from the daily activities of the common people. Anything that deviates from this is a deviant doctrine.

The essence of heavenly true nature is fundamentally, inherently leaping with life. When eagles fly and fish swim, it is this essence.

Love people until people are loving too. Respect people until people are respectful too. Be faithful to people until people are faithful too. This alone is the method for learning without stopping.

Although Confucius was a natural-born sage, even he had to study [the classics like] *The Book of Poetry, The Book of Rites,* and the *I Ching* and gradually polish himself, before his penetrating illumination was perfected.

Heaven's true pattern is the natural, inherently existing true pattern. As soon as you wish to arrange how it should be, this is human desire.

Learning takes place right in the midst of practical affairs. The Tao is right in the midst of practical affairs.

A student commented that it was hard to search for lost mind. Wang Gen called to him and he responded. Wang Gen said, "Your mind is here right now. What else are you searching for?"

If we only know how to safeguard our personal existence, and we do not know how to love other people, we are sure to end up acting for our own convenience. If we benefit ourselves and harm others, they are sure to pay us back, and then we cannot safeguard our own existence.

True humanity means loving others. Being trustworthy means having trust in others. This is a path where inner and outer are joined. From this point of view, if you do not love other people, then it is apparent that you yourself lack true humanity. If you do not have trust in other people, then it is apparent that you yourself are not trustworthy.

You must work on simply being cautious in your own private behavior. Act when you should act and stop when you should stop. This is gathering together righteousness. If you do this, then you will not waver when you encounter situations or engage in idle and false thinking.

The human mind is fundamentally spontaneously joyous. [Trouble comes] when it becomes tied up with selfish desires. As soon as selfish desires sprout, innate moral knowledge becomes aware of them. Once it becomes aware, it wipes them away, and the human mind is joyous as before. Joy is joy in this learning. Learning is learning this joy.

ZOU SHOUYI

The son of an official, Zou Shouyi (1491–1562) placed third in the palace exams for the highest degree in 1511 and was appointed to the prestigious Hanlin Academy. He became a follower of Wang Yangming in 1520.

Zou Shouyi had opposed the wishes of the new emperor in 1522, and the emperor's displeasure shadowed his official career, causing him to be demoted twice and ultimately dismissed from office. Wang Yangming reportedly esteemed Zou for his equanimity in the face of his demotions.

Zou Shouyi spent forty years in private life, teaching.

The basic essence of our minds is pure and illuminated and luminous and aware. It is as great as the constant shining of the sun and moon, as profound as the constant flow of the rivers and streams.

If it is somehow blocked or obstructed, clear away the blockages and break through the obstructions and you will again see the basic essence. The reason why the ancients gave this such urgency and such emphasis is precisely that they wanted us to make whole this ever-shining, ever-bright essence.

The teaching on innate moral knowledge follows the true nature of Heaven's mandate [for mankind] and points to our pure spiritual luminous awareness. Empathy, a sense of shame at evil, deference, a knowledge of right and wrong: the movement of innate moral knowledge is everywhere.

Thus, if we are careful and cautious, we can be centered and harmonious and thereby properly orient and nurture ourselves. If we extend and fill out the starting points [of moral values that are innate within us], we can preserve the whole world.

The way the ancients understood profit and loss was in terms of moral principles. The way people today understand moral principles is in terms of profit and loss.

Where innate moral knowledge is pure and clear, of itself it possesses standards that are natural and definite. When you should act, you act; when you should stop, you stop. As with eagles flying or fish swimming, this is truly the liveliness of the natural potential, from the start without any obstruction, without any picking and choosing.

The thing to worry about is selfish desire for fame and gain. Once these block the purity and clarity of innate knowledge, then chaff blinds the eye, and Heaven and Earth are switched around.

The essential message of the school of the sages is to cultivate oneself with reverence. Reverence is when innate moral knowledge is pure and clear and is not mixed with corrupt customs.

When you are careful and cautious and fearful [of acting immoral], and you always keep [your innate moral knowledge] pure and clear, then when you go out your gate you will act as [polite and considerate as] a guest, and when you take up any task you will be [as careful] as if performing a sacrifice.

Thus, in giving moral leadership to a nation, having a reverent attitude toward things is the guiding principle.

Trustworthiness is unceasing reverence. It is not that outside of reverence there is something else that is trustworthiness.

The early Confucians thought that if [reverence and trustworthiness] are not extended to political administration, then there will be no way to cultivate the self or bring peace to the common people.

To regulate expenditures and love the people, to employ the people with the proper timing: this is how reverence flows into political administration.

The common failing of the conventionally minded is that they only recognize a sage who has ability, achievement, and fame. They fail to recognize a sage who does not have talent, achievement, and fame.

Recently a friend said to me, "The way a morally developed person manages the world is to be concerned only with right and wrong and to pay no more attention to profit and loss."

I replied to him, "True gain and loss under Heaven is precisely what is morally right and morally wrong under Heaven. For example, to sacrifice one's life for moral duty and to let oneself be killed to accomplish true humanity: how could this be considered a loss? To be grossly avaricious and monopolize everything: how could this be considered profitable?"

Our failing is to be negligent with our time. Because of this we never get the use of our careful study and refined learning. [If we are about to slack off] we must act as Lu Xiangshan said: "Block the road and do not let a single person pass." Only then will it be the learning that we do not depart from for an instant.

If we point to the great fairness and impartiality of its shining essence, it is called "balance." If we point to the adaptive responsiveness and unerring quality of its shining essence, it is called "harmony." It is one thing with two names.

In the gate of the sage, to be intent on learning means to be intent on learning not to overstep the guidelines. We lecture on learning so that we can cultivate virtue. But if we overstep the guidelines in our daily activities and are content with our small failings, then how can we be wholly integrated? If there is something within us that we are not at peace with, we warn ourselves against it and are fearful [of continuing in error]. This is constant learning and constant development at all levels.

We consider finding the essence of mind as good fortune and losing it as ill fortune. Contemporary people consider gaining external things as good fortune and losing them as ill fortune.

If we create virtue, then we will be more at peace every day. If we create falsity, then we will be more clumsy every day. Thus we see that the reflections [of our deeds] are not inaccurate. If we dedicate ourselves to material things and compete to embellish our facades, our own bodies and minds will soon go to ruin. No misfortune is greater than this.

Every day we are in contact with human relationships and the material world: we cannot get away from them for a moment. Therefore we must constantly strive to be virtuous in deed and scrupulous in speech, and we must never let ourselves go. It is like someone weaving cloth: thread after thread goes into the shuttle, and no thread can be allowed to break. This is the great principle of the warp and woof, of total consistency in all actions.

After questioning someone suffering from idle thoughts and miscellaneous thoughts, Master Zou said: "You let yourself think idle thoughts, but you detest idle thought. You let yourself think miscellaneous thoughts, but you hate miscellaneous thought. It is as if you were drunk on wine but hated being drunk. If you were truly capable of being mindful of caution and fear [about going wrong] and never departing from this attitude for a moment, then how would you have any free time to let your thoughts go floating off?"

If students really have the intention to seek to be sages, then they must seek to focus their attention on this. This is the basis for becoming a sage.

In learning, nothing is more important than recognizing true humanity. True humanity is the mind of mankind. When we humans were in our natural state, we were purely an embodiment of Heaven's true pattern. Later all sorts of cravings and desires and thoughts mixed in and spoiled us. We must sit quietly and clear our minds. After a long time we will experience and recognize [our true humanity]. Only then can we see our [true] face.

The master said, "Be silent and recognize it." "Recognize" means recognize what it is. "Be silent" means not to rely on hearing and seeing, not to depend on knowing, not to rely on explanations, not to get involved with thought and imagination. Only this is the basic message of the Confucian school. Only by doing this will we be able to be indefatigable.

Therefore, we must recognize this essence. Only then will our work of preserving and nurturing [the mind of the Tao] have a solid grounding.

In learning, nothing is more necessary than sincere conduct. True humanity is not an empty theory. All the details of proper conduct are part of true humanity. We must realize that there is no true humanity outside of practical affairs.

If the essence of true humanity constantly flows through all [we do], then in our daily activities we would not dare to overlook it in important matters like human relationships or to be unclear about it in lesser matters, like our dealings with the material world.

Since as people we are never for a moment away from human relations and the material world, how can we ever depart for a moment from the work of embodying true humanity? If we depart from it for a moment, then we are not truly human, and we should not talk to others of true humanity.

In what he looked at and what he listened to, in what he said and what he did, Master Yan Hui [the favorite disciple of Confucius] never mixed in anything that was immoral. [If we act like this], this is sincere conduct at all times, this is serving our minds well at all times.

Confucius said that if we are intent on true humanity, then there will be no evil in us. If you do not have this true intent, then you may be very busy all day long, but it will all be selfish private motives.

Liu Yuanqing asked Master Zou, "Why are there so many people recently who follow [the iconoclast] Li Zhi?"

Master Zou said, "Who in his heart does not want to be a sage? It is just that people can do nothing about what blocks them from sagehood. These days Li Zhi says that alcohol and sex and ambition for wealth do not present any obstacle at all [to sagehood]. If the road to enlightenment were this convenient, who would not follow it?"

If learning does not lead to clarity in the mind, then conduct will diverge. If clarity is not made manifest in conduct, then clarity is empty. Clarity means clearly understanding how to act. Action is acting out what one clearly understands.

Therefore, clearly understanding our virtue of filial piety is not a matter of transcendent awakening to the principle of filial piety. It is genuine, full appreciation of how we should serve our parents: only then is the virtue of filial piety clearly understood.

If we have a single moment of thought that is truly genuine, and we seek only to recover our true essence, then this moment of thought that desires true humanity is already wholly the essence of true humanity. There is no falsity, there is no conceit. When there is no falsity and no conceit, what is this if not the essence of true humanity? But to fully develop the ability to carry [true humanity] into practice vigorously and fuse everything into it: this can be done only over an extended period of time.

People these days just say, "I have never committed any great evils, I have never had any extremely evil thoughts."

To act like this is a mistake. They do not realize that to pass their days in a state of confusion and stupidity, like drunkards and dreamers, is in itself a great evil. Heaven and Earth gave us life to be human beings. How can we do no more than act dim and stupid here between Heaven and Earth, living on the same level as ants?

For learning, what is necessary is to believe in the notion that all people can become [sages like] Yao and Shun.

Years ago one of his friends asked Master Wang Gen, "What is comprehending everything without thought?"

Wang Gen called to the servant boy, who immediately responded. He ordered him to get some tea, and the servant boy immediately brought it.

When the friend repeated his question, Wang Gen said, "Without any expectation that we would call him, even this servant boy responded immediately as soon as we summoned him. This is comprehending everything without thinking."

The friend said, "If so, then the whole world is full of sages."

Wang Gen said, "[People are indeed all sages], but in their daily activities they do not realize it. Sometimes they are lazy or tired out, sometimes they cheat and do not respond. Then it is not the mind [we have seen in the servant boy] now."

One day Master Wang Yangming was lecturing to his disciples about responding adaptively with great impartiality, but they did not understand him.

He took the disciples for a walk in the fields. There they saw a plowman's wife bringing him food. Her husband took [the bowl of food], and after he had finished eating, he gave it back to her, and she took it away. Wang Yangming said, "This is responding adaptively with great impartiality.'

The disciples were still in doubt. Wang Yangming said to them, "These peasants are making use of it in their daily activities without realizing it. If they become vexed when something untoward happens, then they lose this mind-essence."

People who are great do not lose their childlike minds. Children are true sages.

Human fellow-feeling is something that does not have to be imagined but appears spontaneously by itself. If you have to imagine it before you can see it, this is not true human fellow-feeling.

Human fellow-feeling is something that is settled by itself

without having to arrange it and put it in place. If we have to arrange it and put it in place before it is settled, then this is not true human fellow-feeling.

Human fellow-feeling is something that works without contrived action. Something that works by contrived action is not true human fellow-feeling.

Human fellow-feeling is something that cannot depart from our human existence. Something that can join us or leave us is not true human fellow-feeling.

Human fellow-feeling is something that can operate no matter what our job is. If we have to leave our job before it can operate, this is not true human fellow-feeling.

Human fellow-feeling is something that can never stop. If it can stop for even a moment, this is not true human fellow-feeling.

Human fellow-feeling is something we can directly experience everywhere. If there is anywhere we cannot directly experience it, this is not true human fellow-feeling.

Human fellow-feeling is something all people are capable of. If there is one person who is not capable of it, this is not true human fellow-feeling.

Confucius said, "There are only two paths: human fellow-feeling, true humanity, or the absence of human fellow-feeling, the absence of humanity." If you leave the former, you enter the latter. If for a day or for an hour you do not recognize human fellow-feeling, then for a day or for an hour you are not truly human. Without human fellow-feeling, we are not human.

Master Zou said, "When we speak, to be mindful of integrity. When we act, to be mindful of reverence. Just this is learning."

A friend said, "We also need the basic essence."

Master Zou said, "What other basic essence is there? Integrity and reverence *are* the basic essence. Without integrity and reverence, where is the basic essence? We see that our learning must focus on what is crucial. What is the use of empty talk of the basic essence?"

Real practice is nothing but insightful understanding. Insightful understanding is nothing but real practice. Outside insightful understanding there is no real practice. Outside real practice there is no insightful understanding.

OUYANG DE

Ouyang De (1496–1554) studied with Wang Yangming for seven years. Despite the bias of the examiners against Yangming's ideas, Ouyang De won the highest degree in 1523. Ouyang De had an extremely successful career in the imperial bureaucracy, ultimately becoming ministry president of the Board of Rites and chief of the Hanlin Academy. He died in office.

At the capital, an unprecedented number of students were drawn to him, and he spread the philosophy of Wang Yangming very widely among the official class.

To follow one's innate knowledge in stillness is called centering on the mean. To follow one's innate knowledge while in action is called reaching harmony.

The morally developed person always knows what is right and wrong and does not deceive himself. This is exercising innate moral knowledge.

Innate knowledge can do things without learning them and can know things without thinking. Therefore, even a petty person living out of the public eye, who does things that are not good and will stop at nothing: when he sees a morally developed person, he feels revulsion [at his own bad behavior]. This must be called innate moral knowledge.

Though the average person excuses himself [of his own wrong-doings] and is thus benighted, when it comes to holding others accountable, he is very clear about it. This too must be called innate moral knowledge.

If we are capable of not deceiving ourselves about what our innate moral knowledge knows, if we can get rid of what is not good and return to what is good, if we do not do to other people what we dislike them doing to us, then this is indeed the work of exercising innate knowledge and making our intentions genuine. In this state of mind, we are capable of being no different from the sages.

Innate moral knowledge knows how to be sympathetic, knows to feel shame at evil, knows how to be respectful and reverent, knows right from wrong. This is what is called fundamental goodness. Fundamental goodness has this knowing as its essence: it cannot have an essence apart from this knowing.

The reality of our Heaven-endowed true nature is clearly aware and spontaneous. It comprehends perfectly, whatever stimulus affects it. It has its own inherent structure and true pattern. Thus it is called both innate moral knowledge and Heaven's true pattern. Heaven's true pattern is the structured pattern of innate knowledge. Innate knowledge is the clear awareness of Heaven's true pattern.

The mind of the Tao and the human mind are not two different minds. Our Heaven-endowed nature and our physical-energy nature are not two different natures. The water at the source and the water downstream are not two different kinds of water. As the early Confucians said, all that we see and hear and think and do is due to Heaven. As people, all we have to do is recognize what is true and what is false.

What is called innate moral knowledge is [knowledge of] natural, inherently existing rules. If when we see and hear we do not obscure our perceptive capacities with private biases, this is called exercising innate knowledge with the eyes and ears.

Thus, going along with the natural rules is what is called investigating things and extending knowledge. If we abandon them, we will have nothing upon which to base ourselves, and we will inevitably resort to contrived arrangements and imposed constructs.

If we truly recognize what is called innate moral knowledge and exercise it without deceiving ourselves, then it will be perfectly obvious what is true and what is false, what is just and impartial, and what is selfish and biased. We will never end up mistakenly accepting our own opinions or indulging in what pleases us.

If you consider yourself tolerant and mild and gentle, how do you know that you are not being indecisive and lazy and negligent? If you consider yourself strong and firm and resolute, how do you know that you are not being brash and impetuous? There is not a great distance between being hostile and being aloof, between being obsessed with detail and being very observant. Being too sure can seem like being correct, being compliant can seem like being in harmony. If you go wrong by the slightest little bit, then you get farther and farther from what's real.

Unless you genuinely do the work of purifying and unifying [your innate moral knowledge], unless you really dissolve the sprouts of concern for achievement and gain, how will you be able to clearly distinguish among these things by means of your intellectual knowledge and emotional consciousness?

NIE BAO

For much of his career, Nie Bao (1487–1563) was an unusually effective official. As the prefect of Huating county from 1520 to 1525, he cut out corruption, improved irrigation works, and opened new farmlands for settlement. In the 1540s on the northwest frontier, he raised funds, recruited local forces, and supervised the strengthening of military defenses. He became a high official in the Bureau of Military Affairs and oversaw defenses against the raids of the Mongol Altan Khan.

Nie Bao had met Wang Yangming in 1526 and been greatly impressed. He declared himself a disciple when he learned of Yangming's death, and all through his life he interacted with many of Yangming's other followers.

Throughout his career Nie Bao was known for his ability to remain utterly calm in the face of the most trying situations. When he was arrested at the urging of the grand secretary Xia Yan in 1549, his total lack of rancor impressed Xia Yan and won him his release.

I suspect that in those who think that the mind has no fixed essence, the essence of mind is long lost. Shining bright within, still and motionless, and yet the locus and the foundation for the myriad transformations: this is the fixed essence of mind.

Innate knowledge is fundamentally still. It knows only after being influenced by things. Knowing is its outflow. One should not then consider the outflow of knowing as innate knowledge itself, and forget where this outflow comes from. Mind rules within: it is outside only after responding to external things. The external is its reflection. One should not consider the external response as mind itself and consequently seek mind outside.

Thus, when students seek the Tao, they must start by seeking it in the inner stillness and making themselves still and always stable.

To experience what it is like before [the emotions] come forth is to recognize the original face. Use reverence to uphold it, always preserve it, and do not let it get lost.

When you arrive at this stage, habit-energy and opinions cannot take hold, and within your breast you are totally free. You can thereby achieve a comprehensive view, without having to wait till you encounter events and fathom their patterns to do so.

For sages, there are many faults. For good people, there are fewer faults. For ignorant people, there are no faults. This is because one sees faults only after learning to do so. Those who have not learned carry on in ignorance acting falsely and think this is normal, not recognizing their faults.

Always still, always sensitive to influences: this is the essence of mind. To make sure the sensitivity is timely and to guide it with stillness: this is the work of learning.

The idea of innate moral knowledge began with Mencius. [He pointed out how] a young child, without learning to do so and without thinking about it, knows how to love and knows how to be respectful. [The child's mind] is genuine and pure and clear and unified and acts according to human fellow-feeling and a sense of moral duty. If an adult does not lose his child's mind, he too is like a child, with his mind genuine and pure and clear and unified.

"Perfect good" means the mind's essence. "Knowing to stop" means that only after we stop at this [perfectly good essence] can we be stable and still and pacify our thoughts.

Thoughts and worries and plans and desires: these are the transformations of mind. If you have nothing with which to rule them, they all can entangle your mind. If you take stillness as the ruling principle, then your energy is stabilized. When your energy is stabilized, you are purified and you have no concerns. This is the fundamental state before [emotions] come forth.

But this cannot be reached in a single step. You must preserve a sense of being relaxed and at ease, no matter if vexations assail you or not. Always remain aware of this inner stability and stillness. After a long time [working on this], it will be effective.

Our vital energy has its period of flourishing and its period of decay, but our spiritual awareness is never young or old. If we are benighted or illuminated according to the waxing and waning [of our vital energy], then unwittingly we are confined to vital energy.

To go too far, not to go far enough: both are bad. Being centered on the mean is harmony. When we speak of the mean, this is harmony. When we center on the mean, harmony proceeds from that. Thus it is said, "Reach the mean and that's all," and "Center yourself there and stop."

Our essential nature is fundamentally inherently cautious and careful. As soon as you are lax or lazy, you have lost your essential nature.

All functioning seems to belong to movement, but the ruler of functioning is nevertheless the basic stillness.

The spiritual transformation of being influenced and responding becomes unsteady as soon as you get involved in thought and deliberation. With this unsteadiness, you enter into selfish intentions. You may claim you are centered in the state before [emotions] come forth, but you are a thousand miles away from this.

The sages consider the myriad things as being one body. They feel keenly all the pains and maladies [of all beings]. They go along and respond to them, always following their spontaneous natural potential to respond to influences. When we say that the sages have no sentiments, it just means that in the transformations they pass through, they do not get stuck or blocked.

If there is the least little bit of inflexibility or clinging, this is going against Heaven.

Those who have found themselves are satisfied with themselves because they have found their basic essence. If your work [of self-cultivation] is not in accord with the basic essence, you are either artifically trying to help [your moral development] along or forgetting about it altogether. Neither way is the Tao.

If you artificially try to help [your moral development] along, then a mechanical attitude is born, and the mind of the Tao is forgotten.

Simplicity is something that our fundamental nature inherently possesses. If we prepare in advance and nurture it within ourselves, then wherever we happen to be situated, whether amidst wealth and high rank, or poverty and low status, or in foreign lands, or in difficult circumstances, we deal with whatever situation we are in by retaining our simplicity there. It is not increased when we do great deeds or reduced when we are dwelling in obscurity. We act the same whether we are rich and noble, poor and lowly, in foreign lands, or in difficult circumstances. Wherever we go, we are self-possessed, because we have found simplicity.

The Buddhists have gotten the sense of this very well when they say "an enlightened person is the same wherever he is" and speak of "being always peaceful and happy wherever you stay."

As soon as you feel you are without faults, you have within you an attitude that will bring disaster. Therefore always see your faults and always try to change them.

A real master just wants to reform his faults. Someone who pretends to virtue just wants to be without faults.

When someone is skillful at tricks and deceptions, it is because his maneuvering mind is too well developed, and he has rested content with it for a long time. This begins in a moment of shamelessness and reaches its final form when it becomes a firmly established habit. It extends to the point that he has no thought of recovering his honesty and sense of shame. He indulges in all sorts of perversity and excess and will stop at nothing and has no use for his sense of shame.

Whenever you cultivate the Tao, as soon as you are involved with ambitions and desires and schemes, and [your cultivation] does not spring from the natural potential that is there from birth, it can never be called true humanity.

Someone asked, "How is it that I cannot get rid of idle and impure thoughts?"

Master Nie said, "It is because your habitual mind is too slippery and set in its ways. When your habitual mind is slippery and set in its ways, transitory thoughts come and go on this slippery, familiar road. This is not something that has come to be in a single day.

"If you want to chase these idle thoughts away and get rid of them, if you want to stop them and keep them from being born, they will burst out and break through and again entangle the basic essence.

"Therefore, if you want to get rid of transitory thoughts, you must first seek to recover the basic essence. Transitory thoughts will be reduced in proportion to how much you recover the basic essence.

"The basic essence cannot be recovered without reverence. Use reverence to hold to it and to make the essence of mind strong. After the mind-essence is strong, you will be able to be pure clear through and sweep away [all impure thoughts]."

Luo Yuzhang said, "Learning is not a matter of a lot of talk. Just sit quietly and clear your mind and experience and acknowledge Heaven's true pattern. If you see Heaven's true pattern, then human desires will automatically recede and obey. Follow this, hold to this, and gradually you will become illuminated, and you will have empowerment in your teaching."

LUO HONGXIAN

The son of an official, Luo Hongxian (1504–1564) was inspired by the classics early in his life. In 1529, he won first place in the palace examinations for the highest degree and was appointed to the Hanlin Academy. After criticizing the emperor in 1539 for neglecting his duties, Luo was stripped of his offices and demoted to the rank of a commoner.

In his youth Luo Hongxian had admired Wang Yangming. He studied with Yangming's disciples Wang Ji and Nie Bao.

Students these days, because they have not yet recovered the basic essence, must fill themselves with broad learning, so that afterward nothing blocks them and they seem fully prepared. I am afraid that they are just clinging to a concept they imagine and forcing themselves to follow it.

Only when there are no clever tricks at all is true talent seen.

What is called innate moral knowledge has no room for borrowings, needs no supplementing, cannot be waited for: it is self-sufficient as it is.

It is said, "The mind of the Tao is the flowing of the Way of Heaven. There is no way for human strength to uphold it or assist it."

Apart from the idea of them, inner and outer do not exist. When inner and outer are forgotten, fundamental mind has been found.

To think that outside innate knowledge there exists something called moral principles: this still does not avoid the fallacy of trying to supplement and add to [innate knowledge]. Is this not far indeed from believing in one's own [innate knowledge]? Seeing and hearing have nothing to do with it: the only task is true sincerity.

Innate moral knowledge has guidelines but no formulas. It has clear comprehension but no arbitrary opinions. It has a ruling force but does not grasp or cling. It has transformations but does not compromise. It has complete generosity but is never muddled.

Learning must start in stillness. But it is not right to be partial to stillness and escape into it.

Whenever there are difficulties or unwanted thoughts, you must investigate where they come from. If you cannot undertake this task, then you are like gold that fears the fire: there must be base metals mixed in. You must not let them stay mixed together this way even for a little while.

Except for this, there is no way to set to work to take yourself to task.

When a tree that has no roots is laden with snow and blown by the wind, the trunk snaps.

In general, before you have started on the work [of self-cultivation], you do not know what your own sickness is. And before you are faced with a situation, even though you are sick, it does not do much harm. But when you get involved in human affairs, then you realize that you are sick. But you still do not know the method for getting rid of the sickness. Because the method makes you responsible for carrying it out, you still want to avoid the issue. You hesitate and avoid the issue, so the sickness becomes something that pains you deeply.

Just be willing to have your blood and breath follow your mind's will. After you have a little stability, then you have a place to start. Otherwise, it will be your mind that runs around pursuing your vital energy, not your vital energy that follows your mind and is stabilized.

Whenever we research the ancient and modern [sages] or approach teachers and form friendships, these are all means for reducing desires. Otherwise, what's the use of having broad knowledge and culture, if not to save ourselves from the profligacy of selfishness and falsehood?

Thus I think that if we wish to become sages, we must start from being free of desires. When we seek to have no desires, we must start from stillness.

Energetic practice is the number one truth of the Confucian school.

The source for dealing with things belongs to this mind. If there are times when we do not preserve this mind, then there will be times when we are not diligent in dealing with things.

To share in the same essence with all things means we cannot mix in the least bit of our own private biases. Only when our own selfish biases do not enter in can we recognize the essence of true humanity.

Only when our own private biases do not enter in, can we see the essence of the true nature with which Heaven has endowed us. This is because if our own selfish biases do not enter in, everything everywhere belongs to the natural standards that are as they are due to Heaven.

If the root of desires is not cut off, you will always take your stand on worldly sentiments, and you will be unable to escape them totally.

•

If you find it easy to gather in [your mind when you are] in stillness but not when you are moving, [then] you have already left behind the fundamental and become attached to objects. There is no other reason for this: it is just that you have not concentrated your mind and unified your intent.

You must be centered before [emotions] come forth: only then will you have the harmony of [emotions] being in proper measure when they do come forth. You must be empty and open and impartial: only then will you have the sensitivity to respond accordingly when things come.

Stillness is one. It has no before or after, no inside or outside.

To make this mind forever still and without contrived actions: this is being careful and cautious.

Before there is feeling, stillness is not increased. Stillness is not there only when there is no thought and no knowing. After there is feeling, stillness is not obliterated. It is not that stillness is absent after there is thought and knowing. This empty, aware, un-dimmed essence is what is called perfect goodness.

When we reach the ultimate stillness, we joyfully become aware that this mind of ours is empty, without any things, and extends infinitely in all directions. It is something like the eternal sky, in which clouds and vapors circulate without stopping or reaching an end. It is something like the vast ocean, where fish and dragons undergo transformations without gaps or interruptions. It has no inside or outside that can be pointed to, no motion or stillness that can be separated. From ancient to modern, it all forms a single whole. As the saying goes, it is nowhere and everywhere.

This mind of ours feels for people and exercises true humanity toward them. We are not separated from the people. If there were separation between ourselves and the people, this would not be true human fellow-feeling.

It is certain that we get human fellow-feeling from Heaven. It is because this is so that we can use it to accord with Heaven.

If you make daily progress into the inner secrets of this learning, then even in the midst of multiple confusions and complications, you will naturally find serenity and not trouble yourself noticing and responding to them.

In the midst of complex situations, how do we cope? If in the midst of confusions and complications, we are overcome by things and events, this is unsteady thinking dragged this way and that. If we remain composed and at ease and above things and events, this is the step-by-step approach of stillness. If we respond by being unsteady and vacillating, we are sure to end up making mistakes. If we advance by being composed and at ease, we are sure to take full account of the true pattern of events. This is the test of whether or not we are capable of stillness.

The true pattern is surely in the mind, and it is also in phenomena. Phenomena are not outside of mind, and the true pattern is not outside of phenomena. There is no duality here.

In recent times, students who cling to the idea that mind *is* the true pattern often get to the point where they follow ideas and indulge sentiments and pay no attention to carefully investigating the full complexity [of phenomena]. Since this is not the way to investigate things, they are indeed going squarely against the axiom of investigating things.

To gather in the spirit and return it to one place, to keep it always solidified and collected, to be able to be the master of myriad things and events: this aspect of learning can be fully expressed in just a few words. It also can be understood with just a moment's reflection.

The *I Ching* speaks of cleansing the mind and not letting it be polluted, of preserving the innermost essence and not letting it leak away. Apart from cleansing the mind and preserving the innermost essence, there is no other work [of self-cultivation]. If you fully engage in it, then you will be completely solid: this is the way that [the sages] Yao and Shun were careful and cautious their whole lives.

Selfishness cuts you off from the Tao of the sages. To survive when it is right to survive and to die when it is right to die, to give one's life for a purpose, to perish to achieve true humanity: this is not the selfish view.

In general, you must awaken the aspect of inherent mind that cannot be deceived and make it the master. After a long time it will be pure and clear, and then you will be able to distinguish things clearly. If you just take the intellectual knowledge you use in your daily interactions and think that this is the essence of mind, this will not be able to act surely as the master. It will go wrong and be unable to rescue itself from error.

If you just speak of adhering to rules and do not ask what this mind is, you will be involved in conformism and currying favor with the world, dragging yourself along following others.

To be centered on the mean and not lean in any direction, spontaneously to share the same essence with all beings, to attain this state and preserve it without letting it be lost: this is the practice we Confucians uphold to the end of our days.

Except for the functioning of true mind, there is no talent or strength or intelligence or cleverness.

Stability is the fundamental state of the essence of our human minds. It is the locus of our true nature and life. If we can preserve this sense and not let it scatter, if we make gradual process until it is pure and fully ripe and the myriad things are not enough to disturb it, we have entered the territory of sagehood.

When this mind is clear and bright and is not covered over, then you are not very different from the sages. If you allow no wavering from this clarity, and do not let it change, and do not cling to it, and do not neglect it: this is learning. Just protect it all the time and do not damage its clarity: then your conduct and demeanor will spontaneously correct themselves, you will spontaneously be prudent in what you say, your desires will regulate themselves, and you will spontaneously practice good and stop evil.

Learning takes place right in the midst of dealing with practical affairs. If you do any evil, this is wrong. If you are the least bit rigid, this is wrong. What is called nurturing mind, what is called extending knowledge, takes place right here. Here, the more closely continuous your work is, the more refined your awareness will be, and you will not be altered by the things [around you].

To curb petty concerns for profit and loss wherever you may be is the real work of controlling yourself.

Recognize as the basis the mind that does not pursue things. In the midst of your daily activities, as you attend to things and respond to things, always rely on this mind that does not pursue things. As soon as your mind starts to pursue things, you must immediately gather it back in. Work on this for a long time, and you will gradually become ripe.

When Master Wang Yangming called on people to rely on innate moral knowledge, he did not mean to rely on the intellectual understanding that is before your eyes. He meant this aspect of mind that cannot be fooled, that is, the mind that does not pursue things.

When you feel you are gaining power, just go on with what you are doing. If you feel the slightest defect [in what you are doing], you must turn away from it.

Innate moral knowledge is still and clear. But if we mix in false movements, we begin to lose it, and it is hard to recover. Therefore, we must do the work of gathering it in and preserving it, to fully develop it and always nurture it, before we can be stabilized in stillness and secure in our thinking. When we come forth from this basis, we can always be correct in our responses to the world and never be moved by things.

When you have full knowledge of the rules of nature, you have fathomed the inner pattern of things and events. Having fully fathomed the inner pattern, you have fully realized your true nature and perfected your life. How could there be inner and outer in this?

Nevertheless, you approach the Tao only after realizing what comes first and what comes later. This is the progression of learning.

The [true student] does not delight in concentrating on the inner [for its own sake]: this is the means by which he seeks to act properly toward the outside world. Without this [inner concentration], there would be no prior basis for this. He does not delight in preserving stillness [for its own sake]: this is the means by which he seeks to sensitize his responsiveness. Without this [stillness], there would be no prior basis for this.

Innate knowledge is the source, perception is the stream. The stream cannot help but mix with things, so it is necessary to use stillness in order to purify it.

•

This mind is evanescent and ungraspable but is also solid and settled and unstained by anything.

People who are able to speak and write and explain may be called talented, but this has nothing at all to do with true learning. The path of learning requires us to be able to function in a crowded arena to dispel vagueness, so that the true pattern becomes perfectly clear and there is not the least bit of confusion. Without the lifelong work of nurturing [the mind of the Tao] and guarding stillness, so that we have no doubts about anything great or small, how could we attain to this?

Heaven has bestowed on us a single great task.
But there is something in this we must deeply discern. If we manage this task from within the workings of mind, this is the learning of the sages. If we manage this task according to what is fashionable at the time, this is conventional sentiment. These two are poles apart, but they are the result of whether or not we can benefit ourselves by gathering in [the mind] and taking care with its innermost secrets.

When I had first passed the official examinations, I visited Master Wei Zhuangqu.
Master Wei told me, "A developed man has a higher purpose: he certainly does not consider passing the official exams as the pinnacle of glory. [For the time being] sit in silence all day long, keep your mouth shut and do not speak. This will benefit the work of developing yourself."
I felt frightened by this. To live up to these words was far from easy.
In general, not to find glory in passing the official examinations is to forget fame and status. To forget fame and status is to forget the world. Only by being able to forget the world can one be a true hero for all time.

Worldly Wisdom

If we can consider the myriad things in Heaven and Earth as our own substance, then we will be great. If we can be unentangled by the myriad things in Heaven and Earth, then we will be noble.

If we know the all–sufficient true pattern, then whenever we do not fulfill our portion, it is always because we have been content to indulge in our desires and have not used our talents to the full.

Whenever we slacken our vigilance in our daily activities, our words and conduct will go against the constant norms of Heaven and rebel against human morality.

We humans must establish our personal existence on the impartial level of Heaven and Earth. We cannot put any selfishness there. Only this is standing firm in our purpose.

Because you have had lifelong habits, you are weak and slippery, and it is easy for you to continue in old routines. Now you most totally cut these off. You cannot let them go on. At all times, when these things appear, you must act the master, until there are no more of the old habits in your personal life at all. This alone is the work [of self-cultivation].

All day long we are busily engaged with outer things, using ourselves to respond to them, but without seeing them as not ourselves.

[The original] Confucian learning taught people to seek [the Tao] in real facts until one finds it for oneself.

Later generations have separated inner from outer and divided mind from things. I feel that, since Song times, they have not been quite the same as [the original] Confucians.

Gradually reduce miscellaneous thoughts, and your sensitivity and responsiveness will spontaneously become smooth and appropriate.

LIU WENMIN

Little is recorded of Liu Wenmin (fl. early sixteenth century). It is related that from his youth he was simple and genuine and unaware of worldly guile. He was inspired by the *Chuanxilu,* a collection of Wang Yangming's sayings, and went to Zhejiang to study with his followers. Master Liu did not take the official examinations and refused appointment as a student at the state academy. He did study with Nie Bao.

Every day it interacts with this world, adapting endlessly, but this true essence of ours never arises or perishes or increases or diminishes. Nevertheless, the Tao of all under Heaven has its origin in this essence.

Knowing this essence is called knowing our true nature. When we know our true nature, then all our beginningless concerns for success and profit, all the habits of our physical energy, are revealed clearly day by day and are never concealed. Studying this essence is called studying the Tao. When we study the Tao, then all our beginningless concerns for success and profit, all the habits of our physical energy, are transformed daily until we never again act them out. Only if we act like this is it the work of being careful and cautious and simple and genuine.

If you do not recognize the root source of the myriad transformations, then you submerge yourself in clever artifice and defiled habits. You see everything under Heaven as a welter of countless different appearances. Thus your spirit is blinded and confused, and your whole life is toil and suffering.

Always notice in your mundane everyday activities if you still have things that are not in proper proportion. This is the way the sages never dared to be lenient with themselves for any shortcomings in their everyday speech and actions.

The essence of our minds cannot be left behind for an instant. It has no self and others, no far and near, no ancient and modern. If we can penetrate through to enlightenment here, then we can have the same measure as heaven and earth and be companions to Yao and Shun.

Students lack the determination to become sages, so they are defiled by their pursuits and constantly change their attitudes and make barriers for themselves.

You must have keen insight and wash this all away. Resolve to work harder than anyone else, and gradually defilements will dissipate, becoming fewer and fewer as time goes by, until the last dregs are all dissolved away.

The work of extending your goodness and correcting your faults must never stop.

Among our friends there are many who have determination but cannot accomplish great things. This is just because they are entangled with the clichés of worldly sentiments and find it hard to escape. We must be the masters of our minds, and then all gain and loss and glory and disgrace will not be able to cloud our views and take away what we hold to. Only then do we have the will to become sages and a hope of accomplishing great things.

The human mind is fundamentally in a state of spontaneous harmony. Narrowness, decadence, perversity, vexation make it rigid and stiff. If we remove these sicknesses, fundamental mind will clear, and its harmonious and pure essence will return.

It is certainly a good thing not to let go when you encounter situations. But first you must have a settled purpose. Then whatever the situation and whatever the occasion, you check to see if it is compatible with your purpose or not.

The sages nurtured the people and taught the people, and there was nothing they did not achieve, nothing that was not for the sake of the people.

They taught us to realize the full potential of our minds, to fulfill our capacity, and not to allow ourselves to underestimate our personal existence.

What is fundamentally so is innate moral knowledge. To be careful and diligent about preserving this is what is called extending innate knowledge. Innate knowledge can open up all the world's beings and accomplish all the world's tasks.

The countless tasks are just one single task. That is why the ancients did not use their spirits falsely but just concentrated on polishing their will [for the Tao].

The ancients in their investigations proceeded from the essence of mind, and so they reached the ultimate point in all things. Modern people try to take charge of things from the branching streams, and even though sometimes they inadvertently achieve harmony, they never get power. This is where human talents and customs [nowadays] differ from the ancients.

Our Tao has never been broken off or been continued. It has run through thousands and tens of thousands of generations as if they were a single day. It is just that people are not aware of this.

The spirit should not be employed in vain. We must always understand our own fundamental affair. Though this fundamental affair has never been defiled by anything, all things are contained in it.

The intellectual faculty is stormy: a single particle of its dust screens us off from Heaven. Even the most outstanding people are led into error by it again and again. Therefore learning is a matter of extending emptiness and clarifying the source.

To be able to be unhurried when hurried; to be able not to slack off when relaxed; to be able not to be frightened and at a loss for what to do when frightened and at a loss: this is the learning that returns us to our natural state and transforms our lives.

CHEN JIUCHUAN

Chen Jiuchuan (1494–1562) had a stormy career as an imperial official. For protesting the emperor's vainglory, he was flogged and dismissed from office in 1520. When he regained his position under the new emperor, he cut down on waste in the Bureau of Rites and earned the hatred of many bureaucrats. He was falsely accused, imprisoned, flogged, and demoted. Eventually he was pardoned and restored to office.

Chen traveled widely, lecturing at all the famous academies, and was well known for his power of argument. Inspired by the philosophy of Wang Yangming, he admitted that it took long years of study to understand it correctly.

Those in ancient times who learned acted for themselves [and at the same time] developed a full knowledge of all affairs under Heaven. When Yao and Shun brought order to all under heaven, they fully realized their own natures and fulfilled the Tao of the ruler. In what they did there was never any separation of priorities between self and others.

Later Confucians did not know the learning of nature and sentiments. They began to think that being impartial meant to act for the state and the people and not for themselves. This may be how worthy and outstanding men differentiate themselves from the common run of people, but it is also why their actions and policies do not accord with the Middle Path. This cannot be called Heavenly Virtue or the Kingly Way.

Those who rest content with their base habits often accept them as natural and spontaneous. We must recognize that making ourselves try hard is also Heaven's command. Working to cultivate and order ourselves always involves trying hard and making an effort. But it is all the spontaneity of Heaven's command: we must act like this.

In recent years, after directly experiencing and testing this learning, I finally attained the natural potential. Only then was it the ground of reality under my feet.

There are those who do not accept their real self. All along their views and understandings shift and change. They think they have transcendence, but when it comes to this real essence, sometimes they keep it, and sometimes they lose it.

Thus we know that anyone who relies on intellectual understanding wastes a lot of time delaying and postponing [genuine realization].

From a letter to Wang Ji:

In my daily activities as I interact with people, I trust myself and follow mind and never add any deliberate thought. In this there is also a little bit of thinking and differentiating, but I think to myself that the transformations of innate knowledge actually should be like this. But I never avoid regrets. When I reflect back on it, there is something incomplete, something not right in the way I trust [in innate knowledge]. Can it be that I do not truly recognize innate knowledge?

If you pursue things [looking for] insight and control, without clearly seeing the spontaneous natural state of the flow of the basic essence, then even if you embellish yourself and are intent upon practice, this is surely not worthy of being called heavenly virtue.

[But it is even worse] if you then consider stopping desire and hate as the lower vehicle and extending goodness and reforming errors as the sprouts of falsity. [If you take this position] you will make people in the beginning stages of learning rush to catch a glimpse of shadows and echoes: they will all want complete comprehension at a single word, they will all want to be in the realm where there is no error. Then they will just rest content with their biases and their old habits and think that this is following true nature and following mind. You will make them despise innate knowledge, its pure subtlety, its crucial importance, its knowledge of right and wrong, the means by which we are illuminated and made sincere. Then their wrong will go on forever, and they will be swept away and forget to turn back. This will be even worse than their old habits of being divorced from the Tao.

The basic essence is perfectly good. We must not dare to think that good thoughts are goodness [itself]. If we think good thoughts are goodness itself, then when evil thoughts arise, goodness would surely perish. Evil is there, but the basic essence never stops being perfectly good, the mandate of Heaven.

As soon as selfish ideas sprout, the basic essence is already covered over, eaten away, blocked off. Its basic state of flowing shining awareness is no longer there. Therefore, we must break through selfishness. After this, the flowing aware essence can be fully developed. This is why innate knowledge must be extended: only then is virtue illuminated and personal existence properly cultivated.

Learning to have genuine intent rests with intent itself. We cannot use any effort [to make it genuine]. What is necessary is that the complete essence of innate knowledge penetrate through and shine everywhere, illuminating all around without the least obstruction. Then all thoughts and intimations [of what is about to occur] come forth from this. Only then do we know the indications of the spirit. This is what is called having genuine intent.

Lu Xiangshan [taught that we should] work amidst human sentiments, that is, amidst changing events, to honor our virtuous true nature. There is nothing outside true nature: outside of events, there is no Tao. [The Tao] moves without moving.

Chen Baisha [taught] nurturing the outline [of the Tao] amidst stillness, that is, refining ourselves amidst false and idle thoughts and experiencing Heaven's true pattern. True nature has no inside: outside the Tao, there are no events. [The Tao] is still without being still.

This means that [these two teachings] both return to the same unity.

The mind is fundamentally still but always sensitive. The stillness is in the sensitivity: it is the basic essence of the sensitivity. The sensitivity is in the stillness: it is the wondrous function of the stillness.

The *I Ching* considers stillness and sensitivity as the spirit. Without the sensitivity, the stillness could not be seen.

WAN TINGYAN

Wan Tingyan (sixteenth century) was the son of an official who had studied with Wang Yangming. Wan Tingyan himself entered official life and, in his travels as an education inspector, heard the varied theories of many learned lecturers. Finally he gave up office and retired to his home, where he studied in seclusion for over thirty years, seeking clarity of mind. He is seen as the continuer of the learning of Luo Hongxian.

If a person can deal with things well, this is talent, not necessarily learning.

We must have insight into inherent mind beyond interactions, beyond speech and silence, beyond sound and color and form and energy, and always be concentrated on this. We always seem unconcerned, yet we respond to all events from this [insight into inherent mind] and in every case accord with what is proper. Only this is learning.

Mind is the spiritual clarity of human beings. It is the means by which we can be the masters of the myriad things and events in Heaven and Earth. It has nothing, but it never stops interacting with things. Thus it is said, "Still and unmoving, it responds to influences and pervades everything in the world."

Ordinary people always let their minds float around following things, tying them to practical affairs. They fill their minds with things and events and block off the natural opening, so how can they see the essence of mind?

The work of making your intent genuine is just not deceiving yourself about your knowledge of good and evil and, as always, seeking clear understanding from this knowledge.

We must stop at the proper place in everything, in accord with Heaven's rules: self and others will both be at peace, each having found where to stop. Only this is called stopping [at the proper place]. Extending innate knowledge in all things and all affairs is equivalent to what is called knowing where to stop. Thus, knowing where to stop and extending knowledge are one single work.

To bring peace to the world. The expression "to bring peace" is most subtle and wondrous. If we savor it deeply, it makes us immediately feel content with the scene of stopping in the proper place together with the myriad things of Heaven and Earth, where the One Tao is pure and forever still for all time.

Those engaged in learning must see this scene. As they investigate things, extend knowledge, make their intent genuine and their personal life correct, and cultivate complete order, they must always practice unconcern and not be excessive or biased or fall into particularism. When every person is filial and compassionate, then every person will be quiet and secure and at peace. The waves will be stilled and the wind calmed. Empty and open, without concerns: it is all the realm of perfect goodness. This is what is called peaceful stopping. What great peace!

Whenever the rulers of antiquity took action, they were always intent upon bringing peace. The result was that they brought peace back to the whole world. In later generations it was not this way. [The rulers of later generations] have acted under the control of willfulness and opinion and contrived action and ambition for achievements. Since the waves in their own minds were not at peace, how could they bring great peace to the minds of the other people? They have never even dreamed of the scene of peace and concord among the ancients.

If you always give yourself an ample sense of being calm and quiet and empty and at ease in your daily life, then you will gradually come to see what it looks like before [emotions] come forth.

True nature and Heaven are all mind. Just fully realize mind, and you will know true nature and know Heaven. Just preserve mind, and you will nourish your true nature and serve Heaven.

In reality it is just a matter of preserving [the primordial mind, the mind of the Tao]. But preserving mind is not easy. To succeed you must make a life-and-death decision.

When you have no other purpose no matter how long you live, then the work of preserving mind will be most urgent and most real. After you have preserved it for a long time, there will be spontaneous illumination.

ZHOU CHONG

Zhou Chong (c. 1490–1535), a student of both Wang Yangming and Zhan Ruoshui, was widely admired for his integrity and purity. His career was as a local administrator and professor. While many of the followers of Wang and Zhan divided themselves into rival camps, Zhou Chong stressed the compatibility of the two philosophers' teachings.

A prudent mind is essential to engage in learning. A sense of shame is the key to entering the Path.

Any learning first requires knowledge, then energetic practice to perfect it.

To lecture on learning, you must have your feet on the ground of reality and be equipped with both reverence and righteousness.

The work [of self-cultivation] amidst daily activities is a matter of firmly establishing your intent. You need friends [in the Path] to teach you, so that this intent becomes pure and strong and extends and grows, and you have live motivation.

If for four or five days you do not get the opportunity to have friends teach you, you may feel [your intent] weaken, and you may get into difficulties when you encounter things, and at times you may even forget [your purpose]. Then you should just sit quietly, or read books, or keep active. Whatever you come in contact with, use it to nurture this intent. Then you will feel your thoughts becoming harmonious. But this will never motivate you as much as when you are hearing lectures on learning.

As soon as students understand how to do the work [of self-cultivation], they must recognize what the sages were like, and take this as a standard and a goal. Only then will they proceed with the work from a genuine basis. Then they cannot go wrong.

ZHU DEZHI

Zhu Dezhi (fl. early sixteenth century) was a town administrator acclaimed by the local people. He studied with Wang Yangming and was also influenced strongly by Taoism.

Yang Wencheng asked Wang Yangming, "Intent has good and evil: how can we make it genuine?"

My old teacher Yangming said, "Mind has neither good nor evil. What has good and evil is intent. What recognizes good and evil is innate knowledge. Doing good and getting rid of evil is called investigating things."

Yang asked, "Does intent definitely have good and evil?"

Wang Yangming said, "Intent comes forth from mind. Fundmentally it has good and has no evil. But it moves into selfish desires, and after that it has evil. Innate knowledge spontaneously realizes this. Therefore, the essence of learning is called exercising innate knowledge."

Wang Yangming said, "What people must master in life is learning. What cannot be held back even for a moment is time. Since time cannot be held back, it is extremely precious. If you do not master learning, then you have lost your human potential. This is truly shameful. If you are content to be shameless, and you fail to recognize that time is precious, then, when you get old and have regrets, how you will grieve!"

Someone asked Wang Yangming about the similarities and differences among the Three Teachings [Taoism, Confucianism, and Buddhism].

101

Worldly Wisdom

My old teacher Yangming said, "The Tao is great: there is nothing outside it. If you say let [the followers of] each path take their own path as the Tao, this is making the Tao small. When the study of mind reaches pure illumination, the whole world shares the same wind: they just seek full self-realization.

"It is like a large house that was originally one single room. Then the descendants [of the family] divided their living quarters, so then there was a central room and side rooms. As the house was handed down, gradually they set up fences between them, but they were still able to come and go and help each other. After more time went by, there gradually came to be competition and fights among them, and these grew so serious that they ended up as enemies.

"At first, it was just a single family. If the fences were removed, it would be a single family again as it was before.

"The division between the Three Teachings [of Confucianism, Taoism, and Buddhism] is just like this. At first, each person studied the one that was closest to his own temperament, and so they became separate. After they were transmitted through several generations, they lost their original similarity. Because their followers went off with what was closest to their own temperaments, subsequently there was no communication. Concerns for reputation and profit set in, and they ended up in competition and became enemies. Such was the momentum of events."

What is tightly tied to personal existence and cannot be left behind for an instant is poverty and humble rank. What may be gained and may be lost is wealth and high rank. People are determined to get away from what cannot be gotten away from and determined to gain what cannot be preserved. This is why they are busily working throughout their lives and end up in evil.

When the sages of the past established teachings, the guiding principles were not the same: they just set up their teachings according to the needs of the time, with pure illumination of this true nature.

102

Master Zhu reported that Wang Yangming said, "Friends, you have come here from hundreds of miles away, and you think that I benefit you. I myself feel that I get more benefit from you [than you get from me]."

Master Zhu reported that Wang Yangming told his students, "For a true gentleman, learning is a matter of working on oneself. When slander and praise, glory and disgrace come, not only is his mind unmoved by such things, but he uses them as an occasion to refine and polish himself. Therefore, wherever a true gentleman goes, he is self-possessed, precisely because wherever he goes, he is learning."

XUE YINGQI

After winning the highest degree in 1535, Xue Yingqi (1500–c. 1573) had an official career as a district superintendent, inspector of manufactures, and provincial education inspector administering the official examinations. He studied with Wang Yangming's followers Wang Ji and Ouyang De.

Xue tried to show the compatibility of Wang Yangming's thought and the philosophy of Zhu Xi. His writings include a history of his province, a voluminous work on Chinese history since the Song, a commentary on Sunzi's *The Art of War,* and a treatise on the struggle against the pirates who were then ravaging coastal China.

With the students of old, when they knew something, they practiced it, and when they were engaged in practical affairs, they learned from it. Today's students speak of knowledge apart from practice, and learning outside of practical affairs.

If you dare not be lenient with yourself for a moment, this can be called cultivation. If you dare not speak a single word of false flattery, this can be called being straightforward. If you dare not be corrupt in any interchange, this can be called honesty.

•

The sages established the mandate. Worthy people find peace there. Unworthy people rebel against it.

If the times are corrupt, the people are in distress. If the times are flourishing, the people are at rest. Where are the signs of this? They are found in the customary style of the literati: whether they are honest and straightforward or dishonest flatterers.

Reform your faults and you will always be improving. Be content with poverty and you will have enough to spend.

In the case of the ideology of an age when good order prevails, superior people are in charge of it, so virtue is unified and customs share in virtue.

In the case of the ideology of an age near the end [of a cycle of flourishing followed by decline], inferior people are in charge of it, so virtue is fragmented and customs diverge from virtue.

ZHA SHENGDUO

Zha Shengduo won the highest degree in 1529 and had a career in the judiciary and provincial administration. He studied with Wang Ji and Qian Dehong.

Learning requires returning to the root and becoming like Heaven and Earth.

The transformations of Heaven and Earth flow on ceaselessly, but their solidity and stillness are always present.

All people are fully equipped with the still essence of Heaven and Earth. Even though people undergo myriad transformations as they interact with each other, this stillness always remains.

As it is said, letting stillness rule is the ultimate principle upon which to found human life: all works flow forth from this. This is why study must have its root in the primordial.

The essence of the human mind is just stillness and sensitivity. Creative energy, strength, human fellow-feelings: all these are the essence of sensitivity. Receptivity, flexibility, a sense of moral duty: all these are the essence of stillness.

This natural potential originally comes forth from the primordial. It has no before or after, no inside or outside, no refined or crude. If we can awaken to the intent of this, then sensitivity remains right within stillness, and stillness remains right within sensitivity: both the work [of self-cultivation] and the basic essence are right here.

Some people think, "In the world, changing events are endless: how can innate knowledge know them all? To succeed we must also use inquiry and investigation."

They do not realize that innate knowledge is something that comes forth from our own true mind. When true mind is present, then when we must make inquiries, we are spontaneously able to do so, and when we must investigate, we are spontaneously able to do so. Neither is neglected. If we did not inquire and investigate when it was proper to do so, this would not be innate knowledge.

Investigating things means following the outflow of innate moral knowledge and extending it to our thoughts and consciousness within and to our perceptions and words and actions without, so that they all follow the Heaven-given natural pattern of innate moral knowledge.

Innate moral knowledge is the true nature with which Heaven has endowed us: it is perfectly good.

Emotional consciousness proceeds from innate knowledge, but once it has departed from its root and gets mixed up about good and evil, then it is far away from innate knowledge.

Some students think that to hold to a moment's illumination is the work [of self-cultivation] and that this is the method for lasting wakefulness. When they are still, they get power [from this], but when they are moving, they are plunged into confusion. This is because they have made a distinction between inner and outer.

They do not know that this spiritual awareness originally has no inner or outer, no motion or stillness. It is the true essence of us humans, and it is identical to the subtle reality of the mind of the Tao. Once we see this essence, then nothing in Heaven and Earth obstructs us. There is just this single spiritual awareness coming and going alone.

If we respond to the things that influence us by means of this spiritual awareness, then everything is right before us, and we depend on nothing at all.

To be cautious and wary is originally the fundamental essence. If you have awakening but are not cautious and wary, this awakening is still only an empty perception. If you are cautious and wary but do not have awakening, this caution and wariness is only forced control.

Never to forget the true nature that Heaven has given us and, when things happen, not to let this true nature be obscured by physical energy and habits: this is exercising innate knowledge.

As we respond to influences in our daily activities, though we may go through myriad transformations, the illuminated essence of this mind is not moved by sentiments or changed by objects. This empty and still essence is actually right there in the midst of our responding to influences.

Worldly people do not realize that this mind is originally spiritual, illuminated, and unfathomable. They create all kinds of thoughts based on forms. Thus the spirit is enslaved by forms and cannot let its luminous awareness come through.

If we can recognize this spirit and at all times serve and submit to the spirit and not create disturbances within it with our egotism, then the spirit will spontaneously shine through, undimmed, with its luminous awareness and be perfect and complete and move unimpeded.

When the Taoists speak of "forming the embryo," how could this really be something physical? They mean gathering in and solidifying the spirit: this is called the embryo of sagehood.

From the emperor down to the common people, each and every person has his "Heaven and Earth" and his "myriad beings." For the common man, his home is his Heaven and Earth, and his family members are his myriad beings. If a common man's nature and sentiments are not centered on the mean and not harmonious, if his joy and anger and grief and pleasure come forth and go beyond what is proper, then his home, his Heaven and Earth, is turned upside-down, and his family members have no peace. This means he is not nurturing them and allowing them their proper places.

It is evident that the same holds true for a single town and so on up to the whole nation.

TANG SHUNZHI

Tang Shunzhi (1507–1560) belonged to an elite family that had been sending its sons into official life for six generations. He took first place in the metropolitan exam in 1529 and was appointed to the Hanlin Academy, but his official career was blocked because he opposed the grand secretary Zhang Fujing, and he was ordered to retire from official life in 1535. He returned to office when

Zhang died but then was stripped of his rank in 1541 for criticizing the emperor for neglecting his duties.

Tang Shunzhi studied with Wang Ji. He meditated and investigated Buddhism and Taoism. He led an ascetic life, dressing simply, keeping a vegetarian diet, and going on long journeys on foot. Tang studied geometry, astronomy, and the military arts. He became a noted prose stylist and is credited with renovating Ming literary style. His writings were very diverse, spanning historical topics, military technology, mathematics, philosophy, and Buddhist and Taoist themes.

During the 1550s, as widespread pirate attacks caused a crisis along the China coast, Tang became active in military affairs. He took charge of logistics in several campaigns and also commanded troops in the field and went out on warships to hunt the pirates in their lairs. Tang died on board a warship in 1560 at the age of fifty-three.

Tang's military activities attracted much criticism: the usual place of a Confucian gentleman was not in armor on horseback. He consulted with his longtime friend Luo Hongxian (another prominent thinker in the Wang Yangming school), who told him it was his duty to serve in the military emergency, despite all criticism: "Once you enroll as an official, this body is no longer your own possession."

In recent times those who discuss learning speak of recognizing the basic essence and entering directly with a single transcendent leap, without going through stages.

I am afraid that even people who are above average are unable to do this. In the end, [this kind of talk] only amounts to a theoretical exercise, an intellectual opinion.

The more we delve into Heaven's true pattern, the more we see that its pure subtlety is hard to reach. The more we curb our human desires, the more we see how deeply rooted they are.

Those who think this is easy have never really set to work and tried to do it or have never made a serious effort.

Those who were called Confucians in ancient times certainly did not all think that it could not be called learning unless one disciplined oneself with austerities, acted like a corpse, and became as unwavering in demeanor as a statue.

The natural potential is complete and alive. The ground of our true nature is untrammeled and free.

It is human sentiment to enjoy being unrestrained and to find being bound painful. But people think that being arrogant and capricious is being unrestrained. They do not realize that seeing the natural potential is the real way to be unrestrained. People think that indulging sentiments and misbehaving is having no bonds. They do not realize that reaching the ground of true nature is the real way to have no bonds.

"Be careful!" For those engaged in learning, these two words are truly the spiritual medicine to treat disease. Carefully reflect and investigate. Carefully cleanse yourself, so that selfish views and habit-energy cannot leave their seeds in your mind. This is being careful.

The people in this region indulge their sentiments and act recklessly without regard for their reputations and think that this is being free. The sages are not obstructed by anything inside, and to them, this is freedom. It is a matter of distinguishing between these two things.

Do you think there is any contradiction between being careful and being free? Only if you are careful will you be able to see through to the reality of the flow of Heaven's true pattern. Only after you clearly see the reality of the flow of the natural truth can you be free. These are not two separate things.

In recent days, harried by pain and suffering, seeking life in the midst of death, I have abandoned all the tricks and wiped away all the opinions I have been using for the past forty years. In the pure clarity, I have gotten a little glimpse of the shadow [of our true primordial mind].

Originally it is something luminous and clear and whole that permeates Heaven and Earth. At birth, it does not bring a single thing along with it: this thing originally only brings itself. At death, it does not take a single thing away with it: this thing will wholly return to that [universal mind of the Tao].

Unless we do not hold onto any worldly things in our breasts, we will not be able to see this thing. Unless we abandon all our states of mind and thoughts day and night, unless we do several decades of stainless meditation work, as if we are nurturing a pearl or incubating an egg, then we will not be able to gather in this thing.

When we have completely nurtured this thing, we will stop exclaiming how hard it was for all the outstanding ones in the world since ancient times who went to so many people to hear the Tao.

I have tested this mind. Its natural potential is a living thing. Its stillness and its responsiveness are inherent and spontaneous and do not need human effort. When we are still along with it, when we respond along with it, we are just following this natural potential, just leaving this natural potential unobstructed.

Nothing blocks the natural potential more than desires. If we cleanse away the root of desire, then the natural potential will function by itself without our having to hold onto it. It is the means by which we are still, the means by which we are responsive.

The natural potential is Heaven's mandate. Heaven's mandate is the mission with which Heaven has charged us. In establishing the imperative [to live by] among people, people just establish this imperative that Heaven has mandated for them.

Chen Baisha's saying "In all things trust in that fundamental one" well describes the natural potential. If you wish to seek to be still, you will not be still. If you have the deliberate intention to be responsive, this will not be true responsiveness.

If you recognize that having no desires is stillness, then the true source and the waves are basically not two separate things. It is indeed not necessary to feel an aversion to the waves and seek the true source.

You say that you have no sense of stillness on the mountain and that you want to shut your gate and rest in solitude until your mind's will stabilizes. [You think that] when this happens, then you will have joyous appreciation and be on the verge of being given the bequest.

Please, for now, do not try to seek a sense of stillness. Search where there is no sense of stillness. You do not have to shut your gate. Just search when you are interacting with people with your door open. Right in the midst of the confusions and complications of endless comings and goings, try to observe how this mind is.

Do you view as two separate things the complications or interacting with people and the solitude of keeping your gate shut? If you do, aren't you still making barriers for yourself? Aren't these barriers there because the root of desire is not yet cut off? You should exert some more effort on this.

Recently I have met with one or two Buddhist and Taoists. Seeing how well they concentrated their minds and how painstaking was their work of self-cultivation, I sadly lamented the [comparative] weakness of our [Confucian] path.

Contemporary people want to sit in comfort and attain [the level of the sages without any effort]. They hold onto their customary worldly attitudes of concern for success and fame and wealth and social status, but they talk lofty talk about the learning of true nature and life. Aren't they far from it indeed?

In recent times, the sickness of those engaged in learning is fundamentally that they do not take sufficient pains to seek out and get rid of and cleanse away the barriers of desire.

They use abtruse and subtle sayings with an attitude of putting on airs of culture. These sayings are just like flowers in the sky, and in the end all these people accomplish is to mislead them-selves. In essence, they seem to be matching wits with the Zen people. This blocks the road for outstanding scholars. This style is present everywhere and in many places is called learning. Thus, this style is an extremely serious problem.

To be silent and not speak, to cut off the route of words and opinions, to make those engaged in learning get to the end [of words and opinions] and turn back to the fundamental, until they are dragged back to true reality and work energetically to travel the one road: only this is the remedy that can save this dire situation.

XU JIE

Until rewarded with a low official rank, Xu Jie's father belonged to that despised class of permanent subalterns who carried out the routine work of the government while degree-holding officials were rotated in and out of supervisory posts. Xu Jie (1503–1583) got the opportunity to study and won the highest degree in 1523. He was appointed to the prestigious Hanlin Academy.

In 1530 Xu made a name for himself by opposing the Grand Secretary Zhang Fujing but was tortured and demoted for his troubles. With Zhang's death in 1539, Xu was recalled to the Hanlin Academy and began a steady rise through the bureaucracy, adroitly forming alliances with the men at the top. He won the emperor's favor by his skill in composing the Taoist prayers that the emperor loved.

At length Xu was able to supplant his former patron, the Grand Secretary Yan Song, and gain the top position for himself. For ten years, from 1558 to 1568, Xu Jie was at the pinnacle of power in the imperial state. He won wide acclaim in Confucian circles when, upon the death of the emperor in 1577, he arranged the release of those unjustly imprisoned by the capricious emperor, reinstated officials the emperor had demoted, put a stop to the performance of Taoist rituals in the palace, and cleared away the motley crew of hangers-on whom the emperor had patronized.

Worldly Wisdom

Xu Jie was known as a proponent of Wang Yangming's philosophy and had studied with Nie Bao, a prominent disciple of Wang's who came from the same hometown as Xu. Huang Zongxi said that Xu Jie was too much a man of guile and maneuver to be counted as a true Confucian.

People must be able to be their own masters: only then will they not be taken off by things. Present-day people are arrogant when they are wealthy and obsequious when they are poor. This is because they cannot be their own masters.

To undertake learning is just a matter of firmly establishing your will. Once your will falls, then you cannot achieve anything. For example, take sitting up at night to read books. If you can firmly establish your will, then naturally you will not fall asleep. If your will falls down, then you will immediately fall asleep. This is not because you are a different person.

Will is like the root of a tree. Only when the root of the tree is firmly established can you nurture it. All kinds of learning are things that have to be nurtured: if the root is not firmly established, there is nowhere to apply nurturance.

Whenever people who are doing good stop for fear that people will reject them and ridicule them, it is just because their intention to do good is not genuine and sincere. As an example of being sincere and not stopping, take the worldly people who crave wealth and sexual pleasure. Not only are they unafraid of being rejected and ridiculed, they will even risk punishment to continue what they are doing. What is the reason for this? It is because they are sincere about craving wealth and sexual pleasure. When we do good, we must have this kind of dedication. Only then can we make progress every day.

You should not let your mind get lost, but this does not mean that you should make your mind rigid and motionless. Just observe how your mind is when it moves. If it moves within

113

Heaven's true pattern, then no matter how far afield your thoughts go in space and time, this is in fact preserving mind. If it moves into human desires, then as soon as you think one thought, this is letting your mind get lost.

The empty awareness of humans responds to influences limitlessly: thus the mind is in fact a moving thing. The reason it is said that the mind of the sages is still is to describe the fact that it is always empty and always aware and is not troubled by selfish desires. It does not mean that it is like a lifeless tree or dead ashes.

When we work today on being still, what we must do is apply effort to controlling ourselves. Only vulgar Confucians want to hide away and sit in silence and claim that this is letting stillness rule.

People these days are very respectful toward high officials. Even if they have to crawl in the mud, they do not think this is demeaning. But when they serve their fathers and elder brothers, they become lazy and feel unwilling. This is because desire for gain has permeated their minds.

Before people drink wine, they are clear about everything. After they get drunk, they are confused and forgetful about everything. When they sober up again, they are clear again as before. Thus it is obvious that what makes them confused and forgetful is the wine, and that being clear is the mind's basic state.

Thus if people do not delude their fundamental minds with desire for gain, then there will be no worry of becoming confused and forgetful about things. The two words "control yourself" are the remedy to sober you up.

Knowledge and action are in fact a single thing. Knowledge operates in action. Knowledge is what directs action. Action is what gives real substance to knowledge.

Silent knowing is the main basis. Learning is the work [by which it is realized]. These days people think that things like approaching teachers and reading books are the business of learning. Nevertheless, if they do not have genuine understanding of the mind and just superficially work at the verbal level, they surely will not be able to attain, or if they have some attainment, they will not be able to retain it.

The Tao is the ruler of the vessels [that contain it]. The vessels are the traces of the Tao. In terms of human affairs, all the many forms of etiquette at court and at home are the vessels. The true pattern of respect for the honorable and intimacy with kinfolk is the Tao. In terms of the plant world, the many stems and leaves and flowers and fruits are the vessels. The true pattern that is continuously being reborn is the Tao.

Some say learning is just energetic practice, and there is no need to discuss true nature and life's imperatives and the Tao and its virtues. But it is like climbing a high mountain: one must see where the summit is before one can proceed. One cannot seek to advance blindly. If not for true nature and life's imperatives and the Tao and its virtues, what would we practice?

The guideline we must adhere to according to *The Great Learning* is precisely the mind of true humanity. True humanity means loving all people, whether above or below, ahead or behind, to the left or to the right, and wanting to make sure that none of them lose what is proper to them. Then we will be able to extend ourselves and reach others. As Confucius said, only a truly humane person can love people and hate people. The early [sage] kings had minds that could not bear to see others suffering, and so they had policies based on this. To succeed, those engaged in learning must first of all nurture this mind.

YANG YUSUN

Yang Yusun won the highest degree in 1547 and had a career in provincial administration and in the capital bureaucracy. When Xu Jie was in power, he employed Yang, who was from the same hometown, as his assistant in all matters.

An ancient poem says, "A human life lasts thirty thousand days." But how many people can take full advantage of these thirty thousand days? As children we play and enjoy ourselves and heedlessly throw away ten years. In our teens we study texts, in order to pass tests at school, and hurry toward the official examinations. Here we use up twenty or thirty years more. In this time, how much time do we devote to working on true humanity?

When Confucius returned from Wei to Lu, [among his leading disciples] Zi Xia was twenty-nine, Zi You was twenty-eight, and Zeng Zi was the youngest: all of them were already outstanding Confucians. When we look at them from our present vantage point, what great men they were!

In the present day, by the time men pass the official examinations, they are generally between thirty and forty. Only then do a few of them realize they should turn to [real moral] learning. Those engaged in learning in ancient times learned first and then served in office, so they succeeded in both endeavors. Present-day students engage in learning only after they have become officials, so they fail in both areas.

As for those who attain office at thirty, if they have the resolve to spur themselves on and learn morning and night, and study until they are fifty or sixty, then they are sure to be a bit different from the ordinary type. But if they do not make this resolve, what can they do? They will go on being mediocre forever.

116

In ancient times, when people were first living, in general they were close to Heaven. They could not separate themselves from Heaven, any more than fish can leave the water. Thus, whatever they did was sure to be based on Heaven, and whatever they said was sure to be in accord with Heaven. There was no sense of something below according with something above.

In middle antiquity, the sages used the word Tao to replace this [previous spontaneous harmony]. They wanted it to be easy to understand.

Later people instead went to seek from the [concept of] the Tao and felt themselves separated from Heaven by something.

In subsequent ages of decline, even the word Tao is not recognized: life is disjointed, and error and confusion mix in. People live every day with Heaven above them and Earth beneath them and do not know where Heaven and Earth are. So people have beome small, and Heaven is considered great.

Present-day people are bound by worldly sentiments. They are unable to devote enough time to reflecting back on themselves and understanding their allotment of true nature. When they choose their opinions and their actions, it is just to please the eyes and ears of other people: it has nothing to do with themselves.

LUO RUFANG

As a young man, Luo Rufang (1515–1588) tried in vain to stop the activities of his mind and cut off desires, succeeding only in increasing his inner agitation. He encountered Wang Gen's disciple Yan Jun, who advised him to shift his focus to experiencing true humanity. Luo's mental turmoil dissipated, and he considered Yan his master. When Yan was imprisoned, Luo sold off all his property to help win his release. He cared for Yan during his six years in jail and continued to serve him after his release.

In his middle thirties, as Luo pursued his studies aimed at the official examinations, he again fell ill. This time an old man appeared to him in a dream and advised him that he was ruining his mind and body with overwork. After this, Luo's obsessiveness abated.

Luo at last received the highest degree in 1553 and began his official career. He held posts at the local and provincial levels and in the capital, where many courtiers were impressed by his lectures. The powerful Grand Secretary Zhang Juzheng turned against him, and Luo was driven from office.

Luo retired to private life and traveled widely in South China teaching. His followers were legion, though he never claimed to be a master.

The mind is the ruler of the body. The body is the dwelling place of the spirit. A person is happy if these two are joined in harmony and suffers if they become disjointed.

Thus, babies and children are happy and are always laughing for joy. This is because at that age body and mind are firmly joined together. As a person little by little matures, thoughts become confused, and the result is sadness and suffering and feelings that are hard to bear.

People follow conventional customs and become accustomed to things that are wrong. Again and again they frantically search for things outside themselves, hoping to use these to gain peace and happiness. They do not consider that the more they seek outside, the more they suffer within themselves. They grow old and die without being willing to turn back [from this disastrous course].

It is only people with the basic capacity [for it] who spontaneously know how to look for a road back. Day and night they are agitated [by this quest]. They may hear a few words said by someone good, or they may see words of instruction from the ancients. With a flash of insight, they have an awakening. Only then do they they know for certain that the Great Tao is right in this body, that the [pure primordial awareness of a] newborn baby is entirely in this body, that the newborn baby is entirely capable of knowledge and action, and that this capacity for knowledge and action is fundamentally not a matter of thinking and studying.

When this point is reached, the spirit spontaneously arrives at direct personal experience, and the inner heart suddenly awakens to empty illumination. [At this point] the bloodline of the Path of the Mind of Heaven [in these people] has surely become cleansed and purified.

A disciple asked, "Right now, if I give up everything, then how would I be different from an ordinary person?"

Luo said, "You would be no different."

The disciple said, "If I were no different, then how could it be said to be the learning of the sages?"

Luo said, "A person who is a sage is an ordinary person who is willing to pacify his mind. An ordinary person is a sage who has not been willing to pacify his mind. Thus, a person who is a sage *is* an ordinary person, but since he illuminates himself, he is an ordinary person but is called a sage. An ordinary person is a sage, but because he dims himself, he is fundamentally a sage but has ended up as an ordinary person."

All Master Luo's friends were sitting quietly. All was still and there was no noise. There were some who wanted to ask questions, but Master Luo stopped them. After a long silence he said to them:

"In this time of stillness and silence, clear your thoughts and reflect back. Usually you are moving and in a hurry: now you feel yourself stop and settle down. Usually you are in the dark and confused: now you feel empty and illuminated. Usually you are lazy and scattered: now you feel properly composed. You are letting the innate knowledge of this mind shine through brightly.

"Thus, as you sit, each and every one of you is holding a clear mirror in your breast. I ask all of you to look at your face in the mirror. If your mind is upright and strong, then it is like seeing yourself properly dressed, and your attitude is naturally pure and bright. If your thoughts are involved with sensory experience and vulgar ideas, then it is like seeing yourself with your hair tangled and your face dirty. Not only do onlookers feel ashamed for you and laugh at you, but your own mind is agitated and afraid. How can you have a moment's peace?

119

"This mirror is present from birth. It does not wait for people to look at it but is always itself reflecting on people. You cannot deceive it the least little bit. Thus when you act without integrity or act without true humanity, from the very start you are letting yourself go. When you reflect back, it is so because you realize that you ought not let yourself go. It is not that at first you did not know, and you found out only when you reflected back on yourself. All people have the mind that is ashamed of evil. Who wants to go through life with tangled hair and a dirty face?"

When I count the years since I first became an official, it has been almost fifty years now. During that time I have observed laws and regulations get more and more complicated, punishments get stricter and stricter, and investigations and interrogations get fiercer and fiercer. Whenever I'm in a jail or prison, I observe how it is drenched with blood, and I always hold my nose and cringe. I sigh for the prisoners and say, "Is not every one of these men someone's son? Long ago, were they not fondly cherished in the bosom of their parents and dearly loved at the side of their brothers and sisters?" So at the start they were all good, but they are not all good now. When I see them in pain, they are sure to be crying out for their mothers and fathers, seeking their support. Thus it is certain that they were all good at the beginning, and even now, they are not all bad.

Someone asked, "I am always turning back and observing what is within my breast. There are indeed times when my luminous inner heart is shining with light, but before long I fall into darkness and confusion. There are surely times when I accord with the Tao, but before long I am acting impetuously and falsely. Thus there is no consistency."

Master Luo said, "The learning of the profound people fundamentally has its own vital starting point. Once you deviate from the vital starting point, no wonder learning is hard to perfect. At present you are unable to return [to the Tao] using the spontaneity of Heaven's true pattern. Instead, you only seek it in the shining of the mind's consciousness. Thus [in your present situation], natural reality is conquered by human conditioning, and truth is snatched away by falsehood. So how can you go all day without being false and without scattering?"

The man asked, "So how can I find the vital starting point?"

Master Luo said, "The vital starting point cannot be pointed out to you by someone else. Please just have confidence and trust in the spontaneity of your natural potential in all that you see and hear and say and do. What you have previously taken joy in, the shining light in your breast, and your accord [with the Tao] in your doings: do not take any of this as crucially important. After a while natural reality will spontaneously take charge, and your human side will spontaneously obey its mandate."

GENG DINGXIANG

Geng Dingxiang's father and grandfather were wealthy landowners who kept to private life and did not seek office. Geng Dingxiang (1524–1596) won the highest degree in 1556 and over the next three decades rose steadily through the ranks in the imperial bureaucracy, avoiding the usual pitfalls. He wrote a collection of biographies of Ming dynasty officials and a work on the legal code. He also put together a collection of sayings by the Song Confucian Lu Xiangshan. Geng was friends with many leading lights of the Wang Yangming philosophy, including Wang Ji and Luo Rufang.

The way the world speaks of the Tao is like looking at Heaven through a tube. They think that the little sliver they see is Heaven. They do not know that wherever they touch is all Heaven, and so they are crude and arrogant. They do not know that the proper standards of seeing and hearing and acting are Heaven's norms.

The Tao of the sages goes from nonbeing and reaches being. The teaching of the sages is based on the crude and reveals the refined.

After [the primeval] Three Dynasties, the art of learning became fragmented. For the lofty, there was empty nothingness; for the lowly, complications.

Confucius appeared and advocated the guiding principle of human fellow-feeling. Human fellow-feeling is being human. He wanted people to turn back and find the means by which they could be humans.

[Later], in the Warring States Period, the customary standard was success and gain, calculations of strategy and tactics. Mencius came forward to reemphasize moral duty, and let people know that there were things that should not be done.

From the Six Dynasties on, pure emptiness prevailed [with Buddhism and Taoism], shattering the teaching of names [of rote Confucianism]. The Song Confucians appeared and took up the message of emphasizing reverence. Emphasizing reverence means proper standards of behavior.

After the Song Confucians, the teaching went more and more in the direction of rigid formalism. The genuine potential was buried. Wang Yangming appeared and advocated the teaching of innate moral knowledge. Innate knowledge means wisdom.

From human fellow-feeling to moral duty to proper standards of behavior to wisdom. Thus when we bring out their main emphases, in reality they are all one strand, [being four of the five standard Confucian virtues].

These days they take up [Wang Yangming's teaching] as intellectual knowledge and opinion: they venerate emptiness and sink down into nothingness. I think that in order to rescue them, nothing will be better than trustworthiness [the fifth Confucian virtue] to influence them and lead them back to reality.

The essence of mind is broad and vast, spiritual and wondrous. How can it be held in and imprisoned in the physical heart and in the chest? When they speak of seeking [for lost mind], it means seeking it by learning. Learning means becoming aware. They also say to learn by gathering it in. When you learn, the mind has been gathered in. When this mind is lost, it is lost by becoming dimmed. Once you become aware of it, then whatever touches your eyes is it. Where is it that is not mind? When this mind is lost, it is lost by indulgences and dissipation. Once you become aware of it, wherever you are, it is mind. How could there be any losing it?

When I turned back to my body and looked inside, there was nothing at all there, just this bit of brightness here. Only then was I sure that the reason why people are people is just this shining intelligent essence. This essence penetrates through, and then this bodily existence is our possession. Otherwise, we would not have bodily existence. What's the use of preserving this physical shell?

In recent generations they think that investigation in the realm of hearing and consciousness is knowledge and that cultivation in the realm of pattern and form is practice. These people do not realize that mind itself is the Tao.

Reflecting back on recent times, there have also been many who sink into emptiness and cling to their views. These people do not realize that things and events are themselves mind.

As Minister Wei and I were going in to the imperial court together, I said to him, "Whenever I go to court, if I go alone, I feel fatigued. If I go in together with friends, the fatigue abruptly diminishes. If I go in with comrades who share the same purpose, the fatigue diminishes even more. Why is this?"

The minister said, "Other people are originally joined to us."

People are called people because [they have] human fellow-feeling. If people dispense with human fellow-feeling, though they still appear to be people, with ears, eyes, mouth, and nose, in reality they are not people.

People are moved by the force of habit. Many are fond of indulging themselves. Once they warn themselves [against this],

this is the standard of proper behavior. People are yoked by sentiments and desires. Many get themselves bogged down in depression. Once they feel content, this is happiness.

We humans can progress only if we have a place to securely settle our spirit and will twenty-four hours a day.

We humans act for our own sake with true dedication. Each of us, even the lowliest serf or indentured servant, has something to grasp onto, some way to benefit himself. The worthy people and profound people all inevitably pointed out this defect.

Without sound, without smell: this is the true eternal. Whatever is involved with colors and images and names ultimately disintegrates. This thing that does not act, that does not desire: this is fundamental mind. Whatever tries to expand and spread in the end falls into a pit.

Between Heaven and Earth, there are important matters, like [political] order and disorder, the flourishing and decline [of societies], birth and death, victory and defeat, and there are small matters, like acclaim and ridicule, praise and blame, promotion and demotion, success and failure. All these things are relative to each other.

But in the midst of this relativity, there has always been something without relativity above these things acting as their master. If we humans merge with the turbidity of the relative, we do not avoid cyclic existence amidst creation and transformation.

To be pure and unified and hold to the mean: this is really a simple truth. [The sages] Yao and Shun were single-minded about pacifying the whole country. How could they have harbored any crudity or any impurity? This was how Yao and Shun were pure and unified. A farmer is single-minded about sowing and planting, so he has the purity and unity of a farmer. A merchant is single-minded about seeking profit, so he has the purity and unity of a merchant. It is just that what they have their spirits set on is not the same.

To bring order to the whole country is a matter of using people [properly]. But if your own eye is not clear, you will not be able to judge other people: how will you be able to use them [properly]?

In the learning of the gentlemen of my home area, they generally do not want to make use of ready-made innate moral knowledge. This is because they condemn the errors of those who act crazy and do as they please under the false pretext of accepting innate knowledge. If innate moral knowledge were not ready-made, then how could it possibly be fabricated?

XU YONGJIAN

Xu Yongjian (1529–1612) had a long official career in provincial administration and in the capital. He was a student of Qian Dehong.

To seek [the Tao] from mind is how we seek the mind's sagely quality. To seek it from the sages is how we seek the mind of the sages. People cannot purify their minds, so if they take their minds as their teacher, they will not avoid biases and admixtures. The sages first attained what was the same [as the Tao] in their minds. Therefore, for the full realization of mind, we must get our proof from the sages.

The ultimate good is the contents of the fundamental mind of humans. Originally it lacks nothing, and it does not depend on artificial arrangements. This mind's thought must be perfectly good, just as the eyes must be clear and the ears must be sharp, just as the sun and moon must shine down and the rivers must flow.

The human spirit is of itself able to function in the world and able to transcend the world. Every day our actions and rest, our speech and silence, are joined with Heaven: this is how we function. If we wholly follow our fundamental knowledge and ability, then at the high level we do not mix in our opinions in order to seek to diverge [from the Tao], and at the low level we do not enter in with cravings and desires in order to follow other people. All day long we are empty clear through, and throughout our lives we comply [with the Tao] and respond to it. If we are able to do this, then we do good and work to extend it. If we are not yet able to do this, then we make mistakes and work to change them. After a long, long time we become ripe and purify the Tao of following our true nature. This is how we both function in the world and genuinely transcend the world.

Skin and bones, consciousness and movement: these are what make up life for humans. But beyond skin and bones and consciousness and movement, there is something that always remains shining bright. It is very abstruse, but comes out all the more. It is empty clear through and unlocatable. This is the means by which humans live. To speak of it in general, we call it the Tao. To speak of its most important point, we call it true humanity. When we take it upon ourselves as our task, we call it purpose. If we are rich and high-ranked apart from this, this is external accomplishment and fame, this is in the province of shadows and reflections.

In sum, if we are close to skin and bones and consciousness and movement and do not associate with the shining one, the profound one, the empty one, then our closeness with hair, skin, bones, consciousness, and movement will end, and these will decompose. That which is not associated with hair and skin and bones and consciousness and movement is endless and will not decompose. The one that can decompose is not the pure essence of Heaven, Earth, and man. The one that cannot decompose truly joins in the virtue of Heaven and Earth.

Worldly Wisdom

.

Learning does not have many diverging roads. We just must return to the fundamental. People are people by virtue of the intelligence of their eyes and ears. Their intelligence is from Heaven. Apart from this intelligence, nothing at all can be added or subtracted.

The lofty ones may want to hear the soundless sound or see the colorless color, but how can they escape beyond sound and colors? The debased ones sink down into the sounds and colors of misguided lust, flow away, and forget to turn back. Both [the lofty and the debased] have lost their fundamental intelligence.

[The injunction] not to look at or listen to what is improper is there so that we will be in accord with the fundamental and so see the rules of Heaven. The proper norms are the rules of Heaven; they are not something that could be made by humans.

Our Tao runs through everything with a single strand. If you just understand it and think about it, but you are unable to let it flow through your demeanor and the way you speak, ultimately this is a defect of your work [of self-cultivation] becoming blocked.

Many students like to talk about preserving the fundamental essence. They say, "This essence fills the universe: how can we hold it fast in our hearts? We must constantly study it and contemplate it."

We must at all times take the spirit of all the sages since antiquity and directly understand it through experience. [We must ask ourselves]: What were Yao and Shun like? What were King Wen and the Duke of Zhou and Confucius and Mencius like? What were the later Confucians like? In doing this we are not judging personalities. What we must do is imprint their correctness on ourselves. If we only investigate and ponder one point, how can this be called study and contemplation?

127

People make a lot of noise claiming they are satisfied with themselves. They should obey virtue and delight in righteousness: this is how they can be satisfied with themselves. Virtue and righteousness: what do they mean? Right now if we are modest and deferential in our conduct, we are sure to be at peace. If our spirits are harmonious and well-tempered and not blocked, this is what is called virtue and righteousness. Virtue and righteousness are innately possessed by the true self. Those who find their true selves find the mind of virtue and righteousness.

The process of natural creation gives life to plants and animals. This is all fixed and cannot be altered. Humans have ears and eyes and mouth and nose. These come with birth [by the process of natural creation]: it is the same [as with plants and animals], there is no difference. People hope to be worthy, they hope to be sages: these hopes come from mankind's own spontaneous wishes. From this we can see that the process of natural creation has been very generous with mankind. Can mankind fail to respect this and live up to Heaven's intent?

When someone is a petty man, how could this be his true nature? Early on he begins to play games with his intellect: gradually he becomes accustomed to this, and gradually the habit sets. Consequently he flows into evil without realizing it himself.

Someone asked, "How can learning be uninterrupted?"
Master Xu said, "In learning there is that which changes and that which does not change. When you are in a studio sitting quietly, this is one scene. Right now as you attend a lecture, this is one scene. Tomorrow when you go to court, this is another scene. After court when you return to your offices to conduct business, this is another scene. These are what changes in learning. But the ability to sit quietly, to attend lectures, to go to court, to conduct business: this is what does not change in learning.

"In this, we must comprehend what changes. When we manage to comprehend it thoroughly, then we function responsively without getting stuck. When we can thoroughly comprehend what does not change, then the ruling force [of our conduct] is forever at peace. When the two are joined, the mind-essence is uninterrupted, and learning is also uninterrupted."

In the framework of beginningless time, the human life span is like a single breath. Compared to the myriad forms of existence, human beings are like a speck of dust. But from the point of view of the individual person, this single breath is endlessly long, and this speck of dust is so great that there is nothing outside it. So can students be without the respectful contemplation of the Duke of Zhou or the concern not to waste time of Yu the Great?

Seeking to be truly human in the school of Confucius is identical to "the mean" of Yao and Shun, "the ultimate good" of *The Great Learning,* and what *The Doctrine of the Mean* calls "before [emotions] come forth."

Thus, if you devote yourself solely to seeking true nature, you may become stuck on perfect emptiness, so that your living potential does not flow. If you devote yourself solely to seeking mind, you may become stuck on sentiments and desires, so that the fundamental essence is easily lost in confusion.

Only true humanity covers both the spiritual awareness of true nature and the reality of mind. It joins the primordial and the temporal into one and joins the metaphysical and the physical in a single source. It lets you be solidified in stillness without traces, while your life force flourishes and flows out to fill the world.

When we speak of true nature this way, it is not the true nature [some think of as] dead and still and cut off and extinct. It extends to human relations and the myriad creatures, while its true essence stays profoundly clear and far beyond sensory entanglements. When we speak of mind this way, it is not the mind of knowledge and movement.

Thus Confucius concentrated on speaking of true humanity, and we pass it on without fault.

Wu Yubi said that the three guiding principles and the five constant norms are the original energy of all under Heaven. It is also so for personal existence and for the family. Without the original energy, then the world and the nation would collapse.

Students must know to take the three guiding principles and the five constant norms as important matters. Upholding the guiding principles and the constant norms is the means by which to uphold the original energy. Even if the whole world falls into disorder, if a really great man can take upon himself the important matter of the guiding principles and constant norms, then as an individual he can barehandedly support the original energy.

ZHANG YUANBIAN

As a young man, Zhang Yuanbian (1533–1583) followed his father, a persecuted official, into exile. After his father was allowed to return home, Zhang traveled back and forth to the capital for a lawsuit to clear his name. It is said that his hair was already white at thirty from stress.

In 1571 Zhang placed first in the palace examinations and was appointed to the Hanlin Academy. He worked as an instructor to the emperor and the crown prince.

Zhang studied with Wang Ji but disagreed with Wang's acceptance of Buddhism and Taoism. He put together a collection of excerpts from Zhu Xi's writings to show the compatibility of his thought to Wang Yangming's.

Mind has no movement or stillness, but the work of preserving mind is invariably accomplished from within stillness. Gentlemen at the elementary stage of learning have not been able yet to get a grip on things through stillness, so they want to use their own extremely confused private opinions and falsely put their attention on the subtle wonder of movement and stillness merging into one. This is like riding a boat that has no rudder out into the waves of a great river. Rare are those who do not capsize and drown.

•

You say that by imitating the words and deeds of the ancients, you may be able to make progress toward forgetting things. You think that this is both lower learning and higher comprehension.

I think that by imitating the words and deeds of the ancients and seeking to accord with them in every particular, [your learning will be] what is called "broad but inessential, laborious but ineffective."

Would it not be easier and simpler to pattern yourself on our One Mind? The myriad things and events all arise in the One Mind. Without concerns, the mind runs through all events under Heaven. Without containing anything, the mind runs through all things under Heaven. This is the meaning of a single thing running through everything. Thus, without departing from events and things and words and deeds, you can fully fathom the true pattern and fully realize true nature and thereby perfectly fulfill the command [of Heaven].

The work of extending knowledge is entirely a matter of investigating the starting point of good and evil. Only this is real study. People these days accept all kinds of false thoughts as innate knowledge. Thus, it is wrong to say that [innate moral knowledge] does not separate good and evil.

Always to know when there is anything that is not good: this is innate moral knowledge. To know [something is good] and always to carry it out: this is exercising innate knowledge. Knowledge and action are joined together as one in order to complete their virtue. This is the learning of Master Yan [the favorite disciple of Confucius].

The human mind is seldom without thought. If you try to stop thoughts before they sprout, this is already in the province of contemplating goodness, this itself is a thought. To become a sage by controlling thought is just a matter of not distinguishing in a moment of thought between having concerns and having no

131

concerns. When this mindfulness always remains, this is precisely the study that merges movement and stillness. In this there is no shallow or deep, no before or after, that can be spoken of.

I think that fundamentally there is nothing that can be said about the basic essence. Anything that can be talked about is the work [of self-cultivation]. Only when we recognize the basic essence can we do the work. This is what Cheng Yi meant when he spoke of recognizing the basic essence, then preserving it with sincerity and reverence.

In recent generations, those who speak of learning know only about innate knowledge, that they are fundamentally fully equipped with it, that it is fundamentally perfect and penetrating. They get a glimpse of its shadow and immediately think they have in their hands something they can hold onto. They do not realize that there is the work of being wary and cautious and fearful [of straying from the Path]. They think their desires are natural potential and that their emotional consciousness is wisdom. They think they are at rest in stillness, but their false moves multiply. They think they are empty and selfless, but their selves are ever more solid. Their reputations and behavior are ruined. Is the innate knowledge [taught by] Wang Yangming really like this?

You asked, "What is the technique for being a high minister of the empire?"
I replied, "To have no private biases."
You said, "Having no private biases is not all there is to the path of being a minister. One must pay attention to knowing people. There is a method for knowing people. It is necessary to enact a law that when a man appoints someone, he is responsible for his appointee's conduct. Then when he appoints someone, he will sure to find the right man. When no one is negligently appointed, the empire can be properly governed."
I said, "This is surely true. But wouldn't you say, one should choose men by their personal qualities? Since ancient times there

have been talented ministers and intelligent ministers in every generation, but often they have failed because they followed private biases. Therefore, only after one is free from private biases is one able to know people. It is like a mirror that is always free from distortion or a scale that is always accurate. [When these are used] there will be no worry of inaccuracy [in judging] how beautiful or ugly something is or how heavy or light something is.

"The law [of holding someone responsible for the appointee's conduct] when he appoints someone has been in effect constantly since olden times, but in the end it has been unable [to guarantee that] the right people are chosen. Why? When someone is a morally developed person, then most of those he appoints are sure to be morally developed people. Even if he appoints a hundred people, why shouldn't [the emperor] approve them all? When someone is a petty self-seeking person, then most of those he appoints are sure to be petty self-seeking people. Even if he appoints only one person, how can [the emperor] approve?"

The fault in recent times has been to talk only of innate knowledge without talking of exercising it and to talk only of enlightenment without talking of cultivating it. I must insist that we speak not only of innate knowledge but also of exercising innate knowledge, that we speak not only of abstract principle and sudden enlightenment but also of practical affairs and gradual practice. In general I think this is the message to save our time.

There is no Tao outside of Mind. Some speak of Mind and mean the one that is easily biased and easily led astray: this is not Mind. There is no Mind outside the Tao. Some speak of the Tao as not having its basis in Mind: this is not the Tao. Some split Mind and Tao into two things. Consequently they abandon our fundamental emotional nature that includes joy and anger and sorrow and pleasure and seek in the inexhaustible pattern of things. They abandon our fundamental ability to serve our parents and respect our elders and search in the inconstant changes of events. The more diligently they investigate and the more deeply they theorize, the more arid and irrelevant [are their findings] when they use them to respond to things and interact with people. This is a failing in their method of study.

I have my doubts about contemporary Confucians who are always talking about enlightenment but whose conduct is far from enlightened. These unenlightened ones divide enlightenment and practice into two roads and will never be capable of either.

Wang Ji said, "An ambitious man has a purpose that is great and does not conceal his actions." That is, he acts with a straightforward mind, without covering up anything, without hiding anything. Whenever he has faults, he is willing to reform. This is the true road for entering sagehood.

Contemporary people all speak of cultivating practice, but in the end their intention is to cover over and hide away [their faults]. In doing this they are a thousand miles away from the direct road of sagely learning. Dingyu said, "What is valuable is not to conceal [shortcomings], so we become aware of them and can change them. It is wrong to leave them hidden and pay no attention and cling to them thinking they are right."

We must consider that when our parents gave birth to us, we were completely pure and clean, with just this inherent nature and life. Everything outside us is truly like bubbles on the water. So how can we throw away our fundamental endowment and swirl around unceasingly among these floating bubbles outside ourselves that are going into and out of existence by the moment?

With a good tree, even if you cut away its branches and leaves, the trunk will grow. With a person who is good at learning, even if you take away his prominence and glory, his spirit will remain solid.

Leave disaster and fortune and gain and loss up to Heaven. Leave praise and calumny and what is given and what is taken away up to other people. Take self-cultivation and establishing yourself in virtue as your own responsibility. Isn't this the easiest, simplest way?

WANG SHIHUAI

Wang Shihuai (1522–1605) won the highest degree at twenty-five and entered officialdom. At fifty he resigned from office, cut off all outside commitments, and engaged in three years of intensive self-cultivation until he witnessed empty stillness. Over the next ten years, he gradually awakened to natural potential.

Knowing is the outflow of the primordial. When we call it the outflow, it already belongs to the temporal. Though it belongs to the temporal, forms and physical energy cannot interfere with it. Thus this knowing does not depend on empty stillness within and does not fall into forms and physical energy without. This is what in the Confucian school we call being centered on the mean.

Scholars in later generations often considered the consciousness that falls into forms and physical energy as knowing. This is why they are in the dark about the learning of the sages.

If in the midst of stillness the root of desire arises and disappears, this is because your will has not been firmly set. Whenever a person's will is completely concentrated on something, then miscellaneous thoughts stop by themselves.

People in the first stages of learning have been in confusion for a long time. The true potential of their fundamental mind has been totally submerged and covered by the dusts [of sensory experience].

It is because of this that our enlightened predecessors established their teachings. They wanted people who are just starting out [on the path of learning] temporarily to reduce [their involvement] with outside affairs and stop their entanglement with the dusts, [so they directed them to] sit in stillness and silently recognize the true face of inherent mind. After a long time at this, the barriers of error are penetrated, and the spiritual light is revealed.

When you arrive at the time when it is indeed like this when you are still, and also like this when you are moving, then you can go all day long responding to events and having contact with things and dealing with human feelings and changing circumstances without abandoning [the spiritual light]. It is the same essence, no different from when you are sitting quietly.

How could [the teaching of the sages] consider the ultimate goal to be breaking off human contacts and having nothing to do with things your whole life long, sitting like a dead lump and just holding obstinately to emptiness and impassive stillness?

If we do not make progress in learning, it is just because we do not recognize the real ruler [which is the primordial mind of the Tao]. Thus, even if we say we are learning, we are inevitably relying on theories, and we are doing nothing more than working at being people who have no big defects in the eyes of the conventional world.

[There are people] these days who do no work at all on their turbulent confused minds filled with desire, who will not sit quietly. They nevertheless want to become buddhas instantly using their present minds filled with desire, and they gloss this over by proclaiming that sensory afflictions are the seeds of enlightenment. This kind of poison drags people down and kills them.

There is not much to say about learning. If you genuinely have the will for it, you just realize for yourself that quiet sitting is necessary to investigate the toil and corruption in this [worldly life]. Thus, you must sit quietly. You realize that you lack real cultivation in human relations and in the realm of things and events and that you must apply some effort when you are in action. Thus, you must refine yourself in the midst of practical affairs. Here there is actually no fixed method.

The saying goes that neither "abiding in reverence" nor "fully comprehending the true pattern" should be neglected. In essence, abiding in reverence does it all. When there is the pure illumination and complete awakening of abiding in reverence, this is called fully comprehending the true pattern. These are not two separate things. Even if you research and discuss the ancient and modern classics and histories, this is just one item included in abiding in reverence. Reverence encompasses everything. There is nothing that is outside of reverence.

If you recognize that abiding in reverence and fully comprehending the true pattern are a single thing, then your work [of self-cultivation] will never again stop. If you consider them two different things, then when you switch from one to the other, there will be a break in continuity. This is not the Tao of achieving unity.

This mind is profoundly clear and perfectly empty, empty and open, without a single thing. The mind's basic essence is originally like this. If we can always be like this, this is called reverence. As Wang Yangming said, according with the basic essence is the work [of self-cultivation].

The true pattern has its origin in our nature: it has a [solid] basis. Desires are born from defilement: they have no [solid] basis. Because the true pattern has a solid basis, even if we hack away at it for a long time, it can never be destroyed. Since desires have no solid basis, even though habitual defilements are deep, they can never obliterate our true nature.

There is never a moment when we do not have habit-energy. But if we use our enlightened nature as the ruling principle and are always aware of it, then at no time is the face of habit-energy not visible to us. Since we can see our habit-energy at all times, we do not have to be carried off by it.

·

In learning it is valuable to be able to doubt. Just exert effort little by little on the mind-essence, so your doubt focuses on this one place. When your doubt is focused on one place, doubt reaches its peak; then you will surely open up.

If you just float along pondering theories, then your doubt will inevitably stray from the basic issue. When your doubt strays from the basic issue, then the more you doubt, the more you add to your many-branched confusion.

The name "mind" is imposed on the essence of phenomena. The name "phenomena" is imposed on the functioning of mind. In reality there is just one single thing, without any distinctions of inside and outside and this and that.

What fills the universe is both all mind and all phenomena. The greatness of this mind of ours encompasses Heaven and Earth and runs through ancient and modern. Thus when we say to fully realize mind, the myriad things in Heaven and Earth are all included.

Students wrongly accept as mind the petty compartmentalized mind that is vaguely located within them and wrongly accept as phenomena the multiplicity of things and events mixing together outside their bodies. Therefore they pursue the outer or they concentrate on the inner and do not integrate the two. This will never be sufficient for entering the Path.

Confucians see truly that what fills Heaven and Earth is just the true pattern that is always being reborn. They call this true nature. Those who study silently recognize it and revere it and preserve it. Thus they can be intimate with their kinfolk, have human fellow-feeling toward people, and cherish all beings unendingly. Why? This true nature is always being reborn: from beginning to end, for ten thousand ages, always being reborn. Who could stop it? Therefore, clearly understanding and investigating things and social relations are not forced activities. By doing so we fully realize our true nature.

What those who study work on all the time is just silently recognizing the living true pattern of this mind. When they silently recognize it at all times, then they do not fall into emptiness within, and they do not pursue things outside. Comprehending this one thing, they comprehend a hundred things, without fragmenting their basic endowment.

Fundamentally, there is no way to label our true nature. There is no way to exert effort on it. Knowledge and awareness and ideas and thoughts are all manifestations of our true nature, they are all its life.

Our true nature is the primordial true pattern. Knowing belongs to its outflow. It is the child of the primordial, the mother of the temporal. This knowledge is between essence and function.

Our true nature does not depend on being cultivated. All that can be said is that we awaken to it. Life is the manifestation of true nature: habit-energies are always hidden within it. These can be cultivated [away]. Cultivating life is the work of fully realizing our true nature.

In learning, if you do not know [the proper place] to stop, then you surely will not be able to make your intent genuine.

What does it mean, to know where to stop? Your intent, your mind and your body, the nation and the whole world: all are one single thing. But in this there is the root and there are the branches. What is the root? It is what intent flows out from. What intent flows out from is your true nature. This is perfectly good. When you know to stop at your perfectly good true nature, then intent, mind and body, the nation and the whole world are all strung together on one consistent strand.

Timely practice means to know at all times that the perfect good is the basis and to stop there. It means to restrain sentiments in order to return to true nature. What in *The Great Learning* is called "stopping at the perfect good" is equivalent to what *The*

Doctrine of the Mean calls the work "of being careful when alone." These are not two different things. If you abandon this, then what learning will you have?

Although the verbal formulations [given by the leading Confucians through the ages] seem different, they all directly point at the true face of fundamental mind, without sinking down into emptiness and without getting stuck in being. This is the true learning of a thousand ages.

When nurturing [the mind of the Tao] in stillness, do not think of the past or the future. Just be clear and forget them both. It should always be as if you are swimming in the primordial energy before it divided. You must attain this bliss for yourself. Then your real potential will leap up, and your progress will be neverending.

Abandon the conscious spirit, and it's all the primordial realm. This is not something thought and deliberation can reach.

If students can penetrate through and awaken to this true nature, then whatever was said [by the great Confucians] was just this truth. All written and spoken words are all in the category of descriptions. Do not cling to them rigidly.

[There are some] these days who have not penetrated through to true nature but who impose their conjectures to establish theories. This is always like scratching an itch from outside the shoe. What connection is there?

If you are not clear about your own true nature and in the end pass through life just making up theories, how can it be said that you have heard of the Tao?

The mind's essence is fundamentally still. Thoughts are the functioning of mind. If you truly recognize the mind's essence, then at all times you will always be still. This does not depend on human power: the essence is fundamentally like this.

When this basis is always quiescent, then even if desires try to disturb it, it cannot be done. The response of thoughts will naturally be in proper measure, and the stillness of the mind's essence will be as it is.

Knowing is true nature's spiritual awareness. Knowing [in this sense] does not mean conscious investigation, reflective understanding, or drawing distinctions. It is the empty and perfect pure pervasiveness and pure wonder of true nature, suffused with clear light. It does not fall into being and nonbeing. It can act as the basis of the myriad things of Heaven and Earth. It extends in all directions and runs through ancient and modern. Gloriously revealed, it stands alone.

True nature cannot be divided or put together or augmented or diminished: knowledge likewise cannot be divided or put together or augmented or diminished. What makes sages and ordinary people and animals and plants different from each other is just a matter of whether [knowledge] is clear or obscured [in them]. This is why in learning, nothing is greater than extending knowledge.

Someone asked, "Can emotional consciousness and thoughts be gotten rid of?"

Master Wang said, "For one who has awakened to the mind's essence, emotional consciousness and thoughts are all the functioning of its movements: how could they be gotten rid of? But this mind is empty and open and fills up the universe. There is just this one mind: there is nothing else. Nor does one see any emotional consciousness or thoughts that can be spoken of. It is like water forever flowing without waves, like the sun always shining without anything to block it. 'True nature,' 'emotions,' 'essence,' 'function': these are just leftover words."

Mind is empty and open and is like the great void with no limits. Our daily activities, our words and deeds, our interactions

141

with the myriad things: all these are transformations of the great void.

It is not that we are using an internal mind to respond to external things. If you think that we use a mind within to deal with things outside, then mind and things are put in opposition and become antagonists.

Our true nature is fundamentally without desires. It is just that we do not awaken to our inherent nature and crave external objects, and in this way we create desires. Those who are good at learning have a profound realization of the essence of inherent nature, which is free from desires, where there is fundamentally not a single thing. It is like the great void: floating clouds come and go, but the great void certainly does not keep them. This is what is meant by the saying, "With complete clarity, all the dregs are dissolved away."

If you take emotional consciousness as knowledge, then making your intent genuine ends up as learning without substance, and fully realizing true nature, which is the lifeline of the school of the sages, is cut off.

The great ultimate is our true nature; it is the primordial. When it moves it gives birth to the creative force, which from then on belongs to material energy, to the temporal. True nature can give birth to material energy: true nature is not outside of material energy.

This being so, if we do not awaken to true nature, then we have no means to fuse the dregs of material energy and physical form [with true nature]. Thus we must awaken to the primordial in order to cultivate the temporal. This is called the learning of the sages.

Innate knowledge refers precisely to the knowledge of true humanity, moral duty, proper norms of conduct, and wisdom, not to the knowledge of the movements of perception. It is true

142

nature's spiritual awareness, not emotional consciousness. Therefore, innate knowledge is equivalent to Heaven's true pattern: there is no duality.

From the time they are born, people always seek outside. If we now want them not to be attached to objects, not to be attached to thoughts, not to be attached to the basic root that is continually being reborn, and to penetrate directly through to their true nature, then they will feel disoriented and have nothing to lean on. They will be terrified of falling into emptiness.

They do not realize that through the ages this state of having nothing to lean on has been the place of enlightenment where one can sit securely, the home of great peace and bliss.

"Extend innate knowledge": regrettably Master Wang Yangming gave out this saying late in life, and there was no time for his students to appreciate its meaning deeply. After the master died, his students in general took emotional consciousness as innate knowledge, and therefore, as is apparent in their conduct of affairs, they did not gain power.

Someone asked about the distinction between knowledge and action.

Master Wang said, "The true clarity of fundamental mind is knowledge. When the true clarity of fundamental mind extends through all thoughts and actions and is never obscured, this is action. Knowledge is the essence, action the function: they cannot be separated into two things."

Many students take indulging in sentiments as following true nature, and currying favor with the world as solidarity with beings. They think breaking discipline is not caring about reputation, and not working on self-examination and self-restraint is the joyous stage of Confucius and Yan Hui. They accept empty views as transcendent awakening and think of utter lack of shame as "not moving the mind." They think that losing their [primordial] mind and not seeking [to recover] it is [the sage's final stage of] not having to exert the least bit of effort. How lamentable!

Someone asked about refining oneself in practical affairs.

Master Wang said, "You must know what it is you are working to refine. If you just want to operate more smoothly on the level of worldly sentiments, then you are far away from the Tao."

After you have awakened to true nature, you may cultivate and refine yourself at the level of thoughts and practical affairs. If you have not awakened to true nature and only exert your efforts at the level of thoughts and practical affairs, of this it is said, "You may accomplish difficult things by this, but I do not know that you are capable of true humanity."

True nature has no contrived activity. The functioning of true nature is a spiritual secret wonder always being born: it is called intent. Intent is a single thing, but with regard to its awareness it is called consciousness, and with regard to its movement it is called thought. Intent, consciousness, thought: three names, one reality. The general term is spirit.

With spirit, the important thing is to solidify it. We gather ourselves in and return to the root in order to solidify the spirit. When the spirit is solidified to the highest degree, then it is in an unending state of silent reverence, and it is unified in true nature. Then, whether hidden or visible, it flies up without location and without traces. This is called the unknowability of the sages.

When your learning has not fully penetrated true nature, then inside you cling to mind and outside you cling to objects, and both obstruct you. For those who have fully penetrated true nature, mind and objects are both forgotten, and everything is open and unobstructed.

What you awaken to through genuine cultivation is reality.
What you understand through opinions and interpretations is a
reflection, an echo.

ZOU YUANBIAO

Zou Yuanbiao (1551–1624) entered official life in 1577 after winning the highest degree. He had the temerity to criticize the all-
powerful Grand Secretary Zhang Juzheng and was flogged and
sent into exile as a garrison soldier in the remote southwest. He
returned to office when Zhang died in 1582 but again ran afoul of
the men at the top. He retired from the bureaucracy and remained
in private life after 1593.

Zou was a famous expounder of the philosophy of Wang
Yangming and was active in the reopening of many of the academies that had been closed down by Zhang Juzheng.

In 1620 he returned to politics briefly and was caught up in the
factional struggles of the capital.

Every morning at dawn we can see the sage emperors of
antiquity. In every village and town we can see the pristine
civilization of the early dynasties. Ignorant common people can
carry out the ancient rites. The poor and destitute can recognize
true mind. The old and infirm are all our brothers. All the world's
people are our kinfolk.

Someone asked about [Confucius] being untiring in learning.

Master Zou said, "When you know why you are tired of
learning, you will know why Confucius was untiring in learning.
In the present generation people pursue learning at the level of the
traces of form, and so they get tired of it. The sages learn from
the living potential of Heaven and Earth. Since the living potential
is endlessly being reborn, how could they get tired of it?"

145

Those who are good at managing their personal existence are sure to be good at living in the world. Those who are not good at living in the world are traitors to their personal existence. Those who are good at living in the world are sure to cultivate their personal lives rigorously. Those who do not cultivate their personal lives rigorously are just currying favor in the world.

Students whose will is intent on the Tao must have hearts of iron. The hundred years of the human life span pass like the twinkling of an eye. It is important to firmly establish yourself [in your will for the Tao].

Younger students who do not believe in learning have three defects.

The first is to be preoccupied with passing the official examinations and not to know clearly [the real purpose of] learning. This is like being a wealthy merchant but working as a vegetable peddler.

The second defect is that since many of the people lecturing stray far [from the Tao] and lack talent, students do not realize that talent can be developed from attending lectures on learning. When the basic awareness of fundamental nature breaks through, then when you encounter important events, it is like a wondrously sharp blade cutting through kindling.

The third defect is that many of the people lecturing on learning are false, so students do not realize that truth can come forth from falsity. Since their teachers are false, they abandon their own truth. This is like being in a dining room and not eating.

Someone asked about the similarities and differences of Confucianism and Buddhism.

Master Zou said, "You should just understand the ultimate meaning of Confucianism. It would be useless for me to tell you whether Buddhism is the same or different. What good would it do you just to follow what someone else says about this?"

It is best to get to work right away. If you wait until you arrive home to rest, you will be in a big hurry.

Worldly Wisdom

•

To have great achievements and an important post is not very different from clinging to your position and protecting your salary. Gathering in your mind and settling down in stillness are not very different from going into hiding and avoiding things. Being modest and mild and adaptable is not very different from being pliant and fawning and going along with vulgar conventions.

There is hardly any gap between these things. Unless they investigate the subtle indications that precede actions, few people will avoid damaging themselves and hurting others.

Those who speak of purity are not pure. Those who speak of doing things personally do not necessarily do things personally. Those who say they know about true nature and life do not know about true nature and life. Those who talk all day long about being unified are not unified. Those who talk all day long about being in accord are not in accord.

People just say they must gather in their minds. For this, they must have the main guiding principle.

All day long we talk, all day long we do things: this is the real gathering in. Otherwise, if you sit impassively all day long and cut off relations with people and flee from the world, in the end you will be harried and hard-pressed.

When untoward, unwished-for situations arise, fools think they are being abused, but the wise think they are being honored. When slander comes from all sides, the unworthy think it is punishment, but the worthy think it is a field of blessings. When they are surrounded with petty people, the conceited take it as a thicket of thorns, but those concerned with others take it as a whetstone with which to polish themselves.

147

If you do not have the real substance of being serious and resolute and upright, and you just imitate the actions of those who are this way, you are only cutting yourself off from other people.

I have observed that those in the world who have a little learning and a little cultivation make a lot of noise trying to distinguish themselves from other people.

Learning is actually everyday plain food and drink. If should not be too pungent. If it is at all too pungent, this is far from learning.

Someone asked about recognizing true humanity.

Master Zou said, "When Confucius discussed true humanity, he had only one statement: 'True humanity is being human.' Nowadays we look upon true humanity as something profound and far away. What a strange thing! Our being together in this hall right now is true humanity. Nothing else is lacking. But do not miss my meaning."

Someone asked, "The living potential is openly revealed at all times. But what can I do about not being in contact with it?"

Master Zou said, "There is no breaking contact or restoring contact with the essence. It is in our perception of it that contact is broken off or restored."

The questioner asked, "How can I work on this?"

Master Zou said, "Being able to recognize the disease is itself the medicine. Being able to recognize that you have broken contact is itself restoring contact."

If you have not finished with selfish thoughts, if you have not cut off selfish desires, then ultimately you have never been in a state of stillness, and you have never had entry [into the Path]. If your mind is deluded, then [for you], Heaven's true pattern becomes human desire. If your mind is enlightened, then human desires become Heaven's true pattern.

When you have some friends in your studio, and you are with them without any estrangement, this is returning to true humanity. When you are with your wife and children and servants without any estrangement, this is returning to true humanity. If you abandon the realm that is right here to speak of the whole world returning to true humanity, the farther you go the less this applies to your own personal life.

Some enter [the Path] because they have upheld their purpose: they recognize true humanity, and then their vital energy becomes stabilized by itself. Some enter by nurturing the vital energy: their vital energy is stabilized, and then their spirit spontaneously solidifies.

When the ruler of a nation cherishes true humanity and has human fellow-feeling, then he has no enemies under Heaven.

Preeminence in the world at a given time is not tied to position and rank. Every generation must have those who take charge of this Tao. They are the ones who are preeminent in the world of their time.

The lowly recognize one side, the side of physical form. The lofty recognize one side, the side of the true nature given by Heaven. Who realizes that physical form is the true nature given by Heaven, and that the true nature given by Heaven is not outside of physical form?

Someone asked why those who abide in virtue are resented.
Master Zou said, "These days the teachers who lecture on learning do not realize that they share the same essence as the

ignorant men and women. They just want to abide in virtue. That's why they incur resentment."

The real correct place to set to work is to be looking constantly to see what this thing is that is neither seen nor heard. When you manage to recognize this thing, you will have genuine discipline and caution without having to talk about it.

The lifeline of learning for ten thousand ages is the common possession of all people. Fishermen, woodcutters, farmers, herdsmen: they are all people who are aware of the world. Learning is even present in a boy lifting a cup of wine. If you say, "I have the Tao, but other people do not," then you have lost the primordial energy of Heaven and Earth.

The myriad things in Heaven and Earth all are born from nothingness and return to nothingness. All animate beings containing awareness come without knowing where they come from and go without knowing where they go to. Thus their essence is fundamentally empty.

In our learning, we certainly cannot make arrangements at the level of physical forms. For a time they may be beautiful, but in the end they wither and fall.

Nevertheless, this emptiness does not mean annihilation. Floating clouds arise: black dogs and white clothes are all apparitions within the emptiness.

What we must have is the certainty that this empty essence is not changed by these apparitions. With this, Heaven and Earth are in our hands, and the myriad transformations are in our bodies.

These days certain critics claim that the only thing to do is to enjoy the present. As soon as we speak of self-control, they say that this is a phony contrivance. They say that daily activities, wearing clothes and eating food, are identical to the wondrous functioning of the sages. I do not think so. The difference between ordinary people and sages is vast.

If people truly have human fellow-feeling, they talk with a straightforward mind, and their words are virtuous; they act from their basic mind, and their actions are genuine.

If they do not, they try to force an appearance of truth, and they put on a facade of virtue, but this is all trickery. They may take care with their attire and put on a smiling face, but this is all to win favor with others. They pride themselves on having the tradition of the Tao and think they are nurturing mind, but they do not realize that they are thousands of miles from true human fellow-feeling. When it comes to entering the Tao, they cannot compare to old peasants in the villages who are simple and genuine.

A sense of fellow-feeling between parent and child, a sense of moral duty between ruler and subject, proper etiquette between guests and host, wisdom in the worthy, the relation between the sages and the Heavenly Tao: are these not things inherent in true nature?

Students in recent generations think that knowing right and wrong is innate moral knowledge. But when right and wrong blaze up, they follow along with emotional consciousness and are unaware of them. How could this be exercising innate moral knowledge?

For those who study the Tao, to be in the worldly path can be extremely inconvenient. For those who are not sincere toward the Tao, it is easy to retreat. For those who truly believe that all those through the ages who have found this one knowledge are still standing shoulder to shoulder with them, how can they be isolated?

For those who cannot be independent, who run this way and that looking for someone to lean on, who are looking to be told they are good, it is easy to miss [the Tao] that is before their eyes and to go wrong in their whole life's work.

If students do not refine and test themselves through the great treasury of light and reveal their spiritual energy, then although they may talk about what mind is and what true nature is and what the meaning of Confucianism is and what the message of the Song Confucians is, their words do not reach the true meaning. To always rely on verbal traces and imitate principles is to love to practice petty wisdom.

What we are studying are the words of the sages. If we do not adopt a humble attitude and experience these words directly, then we are insulting the words of the sages.

The spirit of people who pretend to virtue is just engaged in currying favor with the world. Whichever way they turn, they say it is good. They are entirely wrapped up with slander and praise and affirmation and rejection.

The spirit of sages is at peace in the fundamental state of their own minds. They pay no attention [to the judgments of those] around them. They have gone beyond praise and slander, affirmation and rejection, gain and loss.

If the mind of the Tao rules, then worldly sentiments thin out day by day. Then you can rule the world without being pushed around by the world.

If emotional consciousness rules, then worldly sentiments grow thicker day by day. Then you cannot handle your own personal existence well, so how can you manage the world well?

When Shun gave laws for the whole country, he proceeded in his thinking from the interests of the whole country. So the laws could be transmitted to later generations, he proceeded in his thinking from the interests of later generations.

These days people just proceed in their thinking from their own personal interests or the interests of their own families. When calculating right and wrong and praise and slander, they limit themselves to their local environment, so the results [of their decisions] are also [only] local.

JIAO HONG

Jiao Hong (1540–1620) placed first in the examinations for the highest degree in 1589. At first he declined an appointment in the capital to work on famine relief. Then he took up a post in the Hanlin Academy. He made many proposals to the throne and worked as the tutor to the crown prince.

Later in life, in office in the southern capital, Jiao Hong was known for his vast collection of books and became the center of a large circle of scholars there.

Jiao Hong had studied with such prominent figures of the Wang Yangming school as Geng Dingxiang and Luo Rufang. He was one of those Confucians who saw Buddhism and Confucianism as equivalent. He put together a collection of biographies of Buddhist laymen and wrote a work to refute Cheng Hao's critique of Buddhism.

The goal of learning is comprehension of higher things. It is like digging a well: the goal is to reach a spring. If you are not going to reach a spring, why dig the well? If you do not get knowledge of true nature and life, what use is learning?

When we humans deal with practical affairs, though they may be complex and confusing, the key link to them is one single thing. What is called "experiential testing whatever happens" is just a matter of recognizing this one thing amidst the complexity and confusion. When this one thing is in hand, then it is like having a bit and reins on a horse, so it will always go in any direction we please.

This one thing is what Master Yan Hui [the favorite disciple of Confucius] called proper norms of conduct. The work of self-cultivation is simply returning to proper norms of conduct. If we can adhere to proper norms, then whatever we see and hear and say and do is the Tao, and there are no more complicated and tiresome worries.

Yüan Hui [another of Confucius's disciples] did not recognize the source and instead sought from the branching streams. The more diligently he exerted himself, the farther away he got.

Why? People are in the Tao as fish are in water. When doubts arise and our knowledge separates us from it, we feel we are apart from the Tao. If we break through the realm of doubt, then we ascend to the other shore. Apart from having no doubts, there is no "other shore" that we can ascend to.

To serve in office and do an excellent job at it is equivalent to learning. To engage in learning and do an excellent job at it is equivalent to serving in office. Doing an excellent job means to have no afflictions in the mind and to be self-possessed.

People cannot bring order to the world just because they have not found the true pattern of this mind. Therefore, they are thrown into confusion by selfish ideas, and wherever they touch they are blocked. If they attained to mind, then even if they had no intention of seeking to bring order to the world, the basis would be established, and the Tao, the proper moral orientation, would be born. This is something that must be so in the true pattern. As the saying goes, get the basis correct, and the myriad affairs will all be properly managed.

If it were impossible by awakening to mind to bring order to the world, then how would we bring order to the world after all? In that case innate moral knowledge would be something useless.

Proper norms of conduct are Heaven's natural rules. With proper norms of conduct, we are able to see and hear, talk and act; we are able to behave with filial piety, honor the worthy, serve the lord, make friends. It enables us to be [sages like] Yao and Shun, to comprehend Heaven and Earth, to nurture the myriad beings. Each and every person possesses these proper norms; each and every person is one with them.

The essence of our true nature is inherently stable and at rest. This truth is precisely what is described in *The Great Learning* as "knowing to stop," and in the *I Ching* as [the trigram] "stopping." This does not mean forcibly controlling one's mind.

If you know true nature, then in human relations and daily activities, without having to exert effort, you are spontaneously correct. If you just try to check yourself in each particular case and think that you are right, you fall into the clichés of the imitation righteousness of the worldly Confucians, and you are even farther from the Tao.

"Awakening" is the hardest word to say. When people these days are the least bit able to put aside worldly sentiments and manage to get some slight understanding of the principles of the Tao, they immediately claim to be awakened. These are still words in a dream.

With real awakening, everything is completely comprehended. It is like a sleeper waking up and opening his eyes: the myriad images are clear and all details are seen distinctly, without any gradual steps.

An ancient said that the Taoists take pity on worldly people with their cravings and attachments and so use the theory of everlasting life to lead them on gradually to enter the Path. I think it is also like this when the Buddhists talk of escaping from birth and death. Worldly people, because of their fondness for life, cultivate the Taoist mysteries. Once they penetrate through by this cultivation of mysteries, they realize that the true self inherently lives forever. Because of their fear of death, they study Buddhism, and when they achieve Buddhist wisdom, they realize that the true self is basically free from death. [Both Buddhism and Taoism thus use] people's strongest inborn feelings as a direct route for entering the Path.

Someone asked, "Cheng Hao said that the Buddhists simply want to obliterate the constant norms we have within us, and they think this is the Tao. What about this?"

Master Jiao said, "How could he talk like this? [What he identifies as Buddhism] is the nihilistic view: it is precisely what Buddha rejected."

Someone asked, "Cheng Hao said that Buddhists with their principle of awakening can be said to use reverence to straighten out the inner realm, but they lack a sense of moral duty with which to order the outer realm. What about this?"

Master Jiao said, "With [genuine] awakening, there is no [distinction between] inner and outer."

Master Jiao said, "Cheng Hao did not investigate Buddhism thoroughly. Therefore, in what he says to attack it, he generally makes conjectures that are not accurate. He is very much like a judge in a lawsuit who makes up his mind about who is right and who is wrong without having full testimony from both sides and suspects guilt without any evidence having appeared. Who would submit to his decision?"

ZHU SHILU

Zhu Shilu (late sixteenth century) was a noted disciple of Geng Dingxiang. He was a diligent teacher with many disciples in the capital.

No matter what their accomplishments, we must first determine the personal quality of those engaged in learning. They must have the mettle of a phoenix soaring up ten thousand feet: only then can we talk with them about seeking this one great matter.

Otherwise, they are wholly sunk in the clichés of worldly sentiments.

The worst worry is not to energize yourself, to live weakly in one place amidst this vast sphere that extends infinitely in all directions. Have a moment that is pure and strong, and it is like a slack bowstring suddenly being drawn tight. Wind flies and thunder rolls. You are roused to move swiftly and stimulated to lift your spirits. In this way, your many doubts are forgotten, your various desires are subdued, your many activities prosper. What else is there?

The world has been drowning people for a long time. Our sense of purpose is the means by which we can deliver ourselves from this and not sink down and perish in the waves of the world. To steer a boat, we do not let the tiller out of our hands. Thus, there is nothing more important for a person than to hold onto his sense of purpose.

The primordial is infinite. Heaven above, earth below, the past and the present, all move within our infinity. Our eyes look at the myriad forms all day long, and our vision is not exhausted. Our ears listen to the myriad sounds all day long, and our hearing is not exhausted. Our mouths speak all day on myriad topics, but our words are not exhausted. Our bodies move all day in myriad responses, but our movements are not exhausted. What is this?

What's to be done? We do not firmly establish our sense of purpose, and we do not see the essence on an intimate level. We take this infinity and abandon it as if it were worthless debris. Thus it is said, "The universe has never separated itself from humankind. Humankind separates itself from the universe."

Learning is a matter of knowing how to apply effort. If we do not see inherent mind, how can we use our strength?

As an experiment, observe an illiterate bumpkin facing an unfathomable abyss as he walks along a cliff from which he may fall. At such a time, his mind is awake and alert and not focused on any trivialities.

The subtle device for entering sagehood is precisely like this. Otherwise, if you pursue fame and duty while holding to your own opinionated understanding, the harder you try, the farther you are from the Tao.

To see the wrongs of others is the root of all evils. To see one's own wrongs is the gate to the myriad virtues.

If our sense of purpose toward our Tao rises and falls depending on other people, it should not be called a sense of purpose.

As a human being, you must have your body in harmony with your mind. After that, your body will also be in harmony with the world. Otherwise, if your body and mind are at odds, then in all that you do, your body will also be at odds with the world. Harmony means both are in harmony; at odds means both are at odds. Being at odds is the road to misery; harmony is the talisman of happiness.

When you have learned not to have a double standard toward situations, then we see the power of your learning. We would be deeply ashamed if we were respectful with friends and guests but neglectful toward ordinary people, if we attained [the mind of the Tao] amidst the mountain streams but lost it in social situations.

There are not many tricks to being a great person. Just do not lose your childlike mind.

In the gate of power, what is advantageous and what is harmful cannot be seen by the policymakers themselves, but it can be seen from a thousand miles away. In the gate of true humanity, what is right and what is wrong cannot be decided by the participants but can be decided a hundred generations later.

[In judging] actions, we must observe what the ruling principles are. If ruled by the Tao and moral duty, then even the maneuvers of strategists carrying out plans are wondrous function. If ruled by expediency and concern for gain then even the teachings of [so-called] sages relying on mind are just borrowed funds.

For learning, the worst defect is to accept opinion as knowledge. If you are in doubt about knowledge and opinion, then this will distance you [from learning]. Knowledge is born from true nature, opinion arises from conditioning. Knowledge is holistic, opinion separates things. Knowledge transforms you, opinion holds you back.

LUO QINSHUN

Luo Qinshun (1465–1547) had a successful career as an official, ending as a ministry president of the Bureau of Personnel. He had a reputation for being abstemious and always correct, and he attracted many followers. He said of himself that he only saw the mind's true nature when he was nearly sixty, after a lifetime of study.

This true pattern is in the mind. Going from the root to the branch tips, in all the multiplicity of the myriad forms, it does not become chaotic. Returning from the branch tips to the root, it is one real, profoundly clear stillness with nothing else.

What Confucius taught people was the work of preserving mind and fostering true nature. But he never said this clearly, so Mencius did. The mind is the spiritual clarity in human beings; true nature is the innate true pattern in human beings.

The mind of the Tao is true nature. The human mind is sentiment. Mind is one, but we speak of it in these two senses, to distinguish between its movement and its stillness, its essence and its function. Whoever uses its stillness to control its movement will be lucky. Whoever gets lost in its movement and loses the way back will be unlucky. Being pure is the way to discern the precursors to its movement. Being unified is the way to preserve its integrity. To hold to the mean and follow one's heart's desires without overstepping the proper guidelines: this is the accomplishment of the sages.

The empty and aware essence of the human mind originally encompasses everything. But it gets covered over by the private biases of the self. Because of this it is clear only about what is nearby, and it is in the dark about what is far away; it sees the small details but misses the big picture. Thus the teaching of *The Great Learning* necessarily starts with investigating things, to clear away this covering.

Investigating things means complete pervasive comprehension with no gaps. When our work [of self-cultivation] reaches perfection, then we comprehend completely, with no gaps, that other beings are us and we are other beings, all together in one whole.

I think that the subtlety of true nature and life lies in the words "the true pattern is one, but our lots differ." When a being is born, and it first receives its vital energy, its true pattern is one [with all other beings]. After it takes shape, its appointed lot differs [from other beings]. The difference in its lot is nothing but the spontaneous true pattern. The oneness of the true pattern is always in the midst of differing lots.

Many of the illustrious state ministers in the Tang and Song dynasties respected Zen. Some perfected their study of Zen and got the use of [Zen wisdom]. Because their innate qualities were good, their minds were able to recover this empty stillness. Because they also had the accomplishment of studying the ancients, if they did not always reach the mean in their political functions and human interactions, they were never far from it.

People have desires: this surely comes from Heaven. Some are inevitable and unstoppable, some are as they should be and should not be changed. Those that are unavoidable and conform to the rules of what should be: how can they not be good? What is evil is recklessly indulging sentiments and desires and not knowing enough to turn back. Previous Confucians talked so much about getting rid of human desires and stopping human desires because they had to be stern to guard against this tendency.

It is certainly true that the Tao is everywhere. We must accord with its moral principles and have no private biases: only then can we act for the Tao.

Another name for the Tao is "law." There is nothing without its law. If we find its law, then we will accord with its true pattern. This is the Tao.

The breath that people breathe in and out is identical to the vital energy of Heaven and Earth. From the point of view of the configuration, they seem to differ in that one is internal and one is external, but in reality it is one vital energy coming and going. Master Cheng said, "Heaven and mankind are fundamentally not two. It is not necessary to speak of joining them together." It is so in both vital energy and in true pattern.

True pattern is the true pattern of vital energy. We must observe it in the turnings of the vital energy. Back and forth it goes: these are its turnings. When it goes, it cannot but come back; when it comes back, it cannot but go. It is so without knowing why it is so. It seems there is some controlling factor within it that makes it so. This is how the true pattern gets its name.

The true pattern is immanent everywhere. In Heaven and among mankind, it is one and the same. The Tao of Heaven is perfectly impartial, so its responsiveness is constant and unerring. Human sentiments cannot be free of the entanglements of selfish desires, so human responsiveness easily goes astray and has no constancy.

The true pattern is something that does not allow the slightest deviation. If we adapt properly to what it allows, we will have good fortune. If we go against it and depart from it, we will have bad fortune.

LI ZHONG

After winning the highest degree in 1514, Li Zhong (1478–1542) embarked upon a long and successful career in the bureaucracy, serving all over the empire. When he died in office at sixty-four, his lack of wealth was a testimony to his honesty.

Li Zhong met Wang Yangming when he accompanied him as a military advisor during the campaign to crush the rebellion of Prince Chen Hao in 1520, but his thought shows little influence of Wang's philosophy.

In ancients times those engaged in study were sincere and genuine. Today's students are compromisers.

Once we do away with our selfish biases, then our minds are identical to the mind of Heaven and Earth. The sages were sages just by keeping this mind whole.

People need a mentality such that they are not depressed by living in obscurity or by lack of recognition. When we reach this level, then the Tao is in us. Those engaged in learning must examine themselves [on this point]. If there is the slightest sense of being depressed, this is egotism, and this is not like [the impartiality of] Heaven and Earth.

If our minds do not indulge in desires, then when we are poor and lowly, we are at peace being poor and lowly; when we are rich and high-ranked, we are at peace being rich and high-ranked; when we should live, we live, and when we should die, we die. When we get so that we are at peace with fate, this is the Tao. These are not two different things. "The true gentleman's thinking does not go beyond his station": this is being at peace with fate. If we wait until we have no choice and then speak of fate, this is not being at peace with fate.

How tiresome and troubling are the confusions of thought! We must clear them away: only then will we know the real joy of Heaven's true pattern. Worldly people toil endlessly after wealth and rank and sensory pleasure. No wonder then, that having abandoned [Heaven's true pattern], there is nothing they can enjoy. If we are capable of preventing this, then the joy of Heaven's true pattern is with us.

If you do good you get blessings. If you do evil you get misfortune. The true pattern is naturally this way. People must understand this for themselves. If a person follows the great road, he proceeds in peace: what could be better? If a person follows a crooked byway, he passes through the wilderness and cannot be unscathed. This is self-evident.

To treat parents and children as they should be treated: ordinary people are all capable of this. To view the whole world as one family and all its people as one person: only the sages can do this.

Confucian learning is a means to understand the oneness of the true pattern in order to aim for sagehood.

Zi Gong asked Confucius, "Is there one idea that one can practice throughout life?"

Worldly Wisdom

Confucius said, "Sympathy for others. What you yourself do not like, do not do to others." Here he taught Zi Gong to extend his practice to the oneness of the true pattern.

Zeng Zi said, "The way of Confucius is just integrity and sympathy for others." This clearly shows the oneness of the true pattern.

The universe has a single true pattern. It is fundamentally impartial and just. People have their personal existence, so [the true pattern] gets covered with selfish biases. The teachings of the sages are means for removing the covering of the selfish biases of the world's later generations. Once selfish biases are removed, then it [personal existence] opens up to the great impartiality, and the true pattern is one and uninterrupted.

Remove all the idle thoughts and calculation from within the human breast, and Heaven's true pattern is free. What happiness!

It is easy to see whether you have attainment in learning or not. If your mind is free, and you have escaped from concerns for power and profit, and you are tied down by nothing at all, this is real attainment.

Though you talk of being engaged in learning, if you are wrapped up in concerns for power and profit as you look this way and that, there is no attainment, only talk.

When this mind is in equilibrium, you can silently observe the true pattern of the Tao.

Whenever we read the classics and the annals, the task is always to illuminate this mind. Whenever we observe anything or deal with anything, it is always to test what this mind gives form to. Thus, wherever we go, it is the learning of nurturing mind.

164

.

The most exacting work for those engaged in learning is to always keep this mind awake and alert.

Whenever those engaged in learning encounter situations, they should deal with them with Heaven's true pattern. There should not be any misgivings.

When people take the mind of Heaven and Earth as their own, this is true humanity. Functioning with this is righteousness. In the *I Ching* Confucius said, "The Tao for properly establishing humans is called true humanity and righteousness." Mencius said, "True humanity is the human mind. Righteousness is the human road."

LÜ KUN

The family of Lü Kun (1536–1618) was registered in the artisan class, but by his time they had accumulated considerable landholdings, and Lü was able to get the education that prepared him for the official examinations. He won the provincial degree in 1561 and, after three unsuccessful attempts, the highest degree in 1574.

Lü served in the Bureau of Personnel for nine years and later wrote of the breakdown of respect and the spread of avarice and malice he witnessed in officialdom. From 1589 to 1594 he was an official in the northwest, where he was celebrated for his accomplishments in building up supplies, strengthening defenses, and providing relief and vocational training for the indigent. While a censor in the capital, Lü Kun wrote memorials to the throne warning of the impending dangers that were soon to engulf the empire.

Lü Kun wrote on many subjects, including medicine and military defense matters as well as philosophical questions. His essays on the duties of officials were put together to form a handbook of practical administration. He was also the author of a famous book of instructions for women and a primer for children.

The primal energy has lasted for millions and billions of years. It is never destroyed. It is the ancestor of the transformations of form and the transformations of energies.

The Tao is the true pattern that everyone and everything in the world, ancient and modern, has in common. Every person has a share of it. The Tao is not selfish and partial.

The sages did not consider the Tao their private possession, but [today's self-styled] Confucian scholars always do. They claim that with the Tao of the sages, one's words must follow the classics and one's deeds must be modeled on the ancients. They say that this is protecting the Tao. Alas! This has been a great barrier through the ages: who will dare to break through it?

The Tao has no shoreline. It is not something that can be limited to the words of the sages. In practical matters, there is the trend of the times: this is not something that the regulations of the sages could fully anticipate.

If in later ages people of clear understanding come forth, they can discover things that the sages did not discover and still be in tacit accord with the intention the sages would have wanted to express. They can do things that the sages did not do and still be in perfect harmony with what the sages surely would have done. This is surely something that the sages would have been very happy with but that hidebound Confucians are very alarmed by.

Someone said that the Tao of the Mean, the mind transmitted by [the sages] Yao and Shun, must surely have some extremely mysterious, extremely subtle inner design.

I sighed and said, "Just in terms of what the two of us have before our eyes right now: if this wine we are drinking is unlimited in quantity, but we do not drink too much, this is the mean of drinking. When we are talking, if we do not keep our mouths shut, and if we do not walk wildly, then this is the mean of talking. When we are saluting each other, if we do not take too much trouble, and if we do not act too casual, if we are neither too quick or too slow, this is the mean of saluting each other. To act like this is to be Yao and Shun in regard to one particular thing. If we extend this idea to the myriad things, it is the same way for all of them. When we reach that place of peaceful action, this is the complete Yao and Shun."

The physical form and the spirit are never apart for an instant. The Tao and its vessels are never without each other for an instant.

When the farmer plows and winnows, when his wife lights the stove and cooks, there is always an inner pattern of spiritual transformation, of true nature and life: they can always reach the ultimate of spiritual transformations, of true nature and life.

Scholars look upon spiritual transformations of true nature and life as something terribly mysterious, and they look upon the things and events of daily life as terribly crude. This is because they do not understand. If they could understand, then they would know that what extends in all directions, what is above them and in front of them, what they walk on and sit on, is all the spiritual transformations of true nature and life.

Someone asked, "What is your path?"

Master Lü said, "When hungry I eat, when thirsty I drink, when tired I sleep, when I awaken I get up, in winter I sit by the stove, in summer I fan myself, when I'm happy I sing, when I'm sad I cry. It's like this, that's all."

The questioner said, "Who could not carry out such a path?"

Master Lü said, "I still have one who has not been able to do this his whole life."

Modern people are not as good as the ancients, because they have no learning and no knowledge. Learning and knowledge must come from high antiquity, before the earliest dynasties: only then can they be correct and great, centered and balanced. These days we just take the opinions that have come down to us since the Qin and Han dynasties and fight to the death with people over right and wrong. This is already ridiculous. It is even more ridiculous to accept the perceptions that are before our eyes and our own intelligence and act proud and refuse to defer to others.

People these days play false in everything. They just carry out their tasks in a perfunctory way under false facades. They will never taste the flavor of reality.

Learning comes from outside. Though the inner pattern of learning is complete in our minds, when it comes to the actual practice of learning, all the famous people, ancient and modern, have studied with everyone and inquired about everything; they have gathered together all the particulars and put them in order, synthesized them and connected them: only after this is this mind in perfect accord with the Tao, and content and happy.

If you are too lazy to study the ancients and too embarrassed to inquire from people, and you try to produce learning from out of your own intelligence, this is pitiable, this is laughable: you don't know what to call learning.

"To act without contrived action." These five words are the root source of the learning of the sages. If students want to enter [the Path], they should set to work on this.

These days when people talk, by the second or third sentence they have already fallen into contrived activity. It is like this as soon as they open their mouths because they have not gotten free of their concerns for slander and praise, for profit and loss.

If you read the intimate, cogent words of the ancients with a crude, negligent mind; if you read the serene, profound words of the ancients with an agitated, impatient mind; if you read the abstruse and subtle words of the ancients with a fickle, drifting mind; if you read the broad and harmonious words of the ancients with a shallow, narrow mind; if you offer criticisms and emenda-

168

tions before you even understand the meaning of the words or read the sentences accurately: you are a real muddlehead.

Each of us has biases that it seems we cannot change no matter how hard we try and habits that have become fully developed sicknesses that will not let us be free. What we need is to have a vehement will that really hates them and continuous effort to keep checking up on them at all times. Altogether, nothing is better than being completely absorbed in the work of nurturing [the mind of the Tao]. After a long time at this, the roots of the sickness will spontaneously be dissolved away.

Nurturing [the mind of the Tao] is ninety percent of the task. Examining [our conduct] is only ten percent. Without nurturing [the mind of the Tao], even if we can examine [our conduct], we will lack the strength to subdue those selfish desires.

If we are careful in what we say and do when we are with our wives and children and servants, and we check on our bodies and minds when we are eating and resting and going about our daily tasks, then this work [of self-cultivation] is completely continuous [as it should be].

This body must be fused with the world. We do not see the forms and traces of the myriad things and the space extending in all directions [as external to ourselves]. This is called transformation. But within this [fusion], things are not blurred: each thing has its own proper pattern of truth. This is called pure accuracy.

All people and all things in Heaven and Earth are originally a single body, a single heart. When we see them as different, they are myriad kinds.

Someone asked about the Tao of reverence.
Master Lü said, "To be correct and composed on the outside and serious and correctly balanced on the inside: this is the

reverence of nurturing [the mind] in stillness. When reading, to have the mind focused on reading; when attending to affairs, to have the mind focused on what you are attending to: this is the reverence of making oneness rule and not departing from it. To act as if meeting with an important guest whenever you come out of your gate, to act as if you are performing a holy sacrifice when you are employing people: this is the reverence of being careful with what you are doing.

"If your mind does not flow into misguided byways, and your actions do not cheat on moral duty, [then even if you act informally], it will not damage your reverence. If you look for reverence only in being formal, [consider this:] all the sages and worthy people of ancient times did menial things like carry hoes and lift baskets of earth, hold the reins and drive carriages. They certainly did not always maintain a solemn pose day in and day out.

"If in general your mind is based on what is correct and your action accords with the Tao, then even if you are not a rigid stickler for formality, it will not damage your reverence. If your mind wanders far afield pursuing a hundred desires, while your body remains stiff and formal, is this reverence or not?"

The myriad sicknesses of those engaged in study can definitively be cured by stillness. The realm of stillness is as large as all of space. Inside, it is perfectly empty and tranquil, without a single thing. As soon as we ask anything of it, everything is sufficient, everything is there.

If this mind does not become confused in the midst of thousands of complications and disturbances, if this vital energy does not stir amidst thousands of vexations and adversities, this is called perfect stillness.

It is difficult to subdue the world, to control the world. But people from ancient times to the present have managed to do it, so it should not be considered the most difficult thing of all. The most difficult thing is to subdue and control oneself. It was this that the sages worked on.

Worldly Wisdom

Innate knowledge of heavenly virtue is the one mind of the thousand sages, the one Tao of ten thousand ages, the thing that sits in a tiny room and still permeates all of space. As soon as we fall into hearing and seeing, there are biases and mix-ups and the odor of worldly conventions. Therefore the sages used what they heard and saw to attest to mind; they did not make mind follow hearing and seeing.

Utter a single word, and there are pitfalls on either side. Speak happily, and it may be taken as arrogance. Speak sadly, and it may be taken as weakness. Speak humbly, and it may be taken as currying favor. Speak forthrightly, and it may be taken as cruel. Speak subtly, and it may be taken as dangerous. Speak clearly, and it may be taken as superficial. Unintentionally violate a taboo, and people will think it was deliberate. Say something uncontrived, and people will think it was a contrived statement.

To speak simply and fit the situation, to speak in a roundabout way and fit the feelings, to speak in a refined way and match the inner pattern, to speak accurately and suit the occasion, to fix the situation with one word, to convince people with one word, to clarify the Tao with one word: this is being good at crafting one's expressions. Two things are necessary for this: clarifying the mind and stabilizing the vital energy.

The world likes to say there are no good people. This is a foolish statement. We do not have to pick out [special] people. From the dense crowd that fills the city streets, gather together a hundred people and take what each is good at. Everyone must have one good point. Collect together the good points of a hundred people, and you can make a worthy person from this. Everyone must have one perception. Collect together the perceptions of a hundred people, and you can decide upon a great plan. When I am among a hundred people, I do not necessarily surpass them all: so how can I neglect the ordinary men and women?

If we can always see that we ourselves are not necessarily right, and other people are not necessarily wrong, then we will always make progress. If we can see that there is always something worth emulating in other people, and that we ourselves have many faults, then we will always make progress.

As we check our behavior every day, we must see if this wish comes from our virtuous true nature, or if it comes from our vital energy and material body, from conditioned consciousness, from material desires. If we examine ourselves like this, after a long time we will spontaneously recognize the original face.

Also in Shambhala Dragon Editions

·

The Art of War, by Sun Tzu. Translated by Thomas Cleary.

Bodhisattva of Compassion: The Mystical Tradition of Kuan Yin, by John Blofeld.

Buddha in the Palm of Your Hand, by Ösel Tendzin. Foreword by Chögyam Trungpa.

The Buddhist I Ching, by Chih-hsu Ou-i. Translated by Thomas Cleary.

Cutting Through Spiritual Materialism, by Chögyam Trungpa.

Dakini Teachings: Padmasambhava's Oral Instructions to Lady Tsogyal, by Padmasambhava. Translated by Erik Pema Kunsang.

The Dawn of Tantra, by Herbert V. Guenther & Chögyam Trungpa.

The Diamond Sutra and The Sutra of Hui-neng. Translated by A. F. Price and Wong Mou-lam. Forewords by W. Y. Evans-Wentz & Christmas Humphreys.

The Experience of Insight: A Simple and Direct Guide to Buddhist Meditation, by Joseph Goldstein.

Glimpses of Abhidharma, by Chögyam Trungpa.

The Heart of Awareness: A Translation of the Ashtavakra Gita. Translated by Thomas Byrom.

The Hundred Thousand Songs of Milarepa (two volumes). Translated by Garma C. C. Chang.

I Ching: The Tao of Organization, by Cheng Yi. Translated by Thomas Cleary.

I Ching Mandalas: A Program of Study for The Book of Changes. Translated & edited by Thomas Cleary.

Mastering the Art of War, by Zhuge Liang & Liu Ji. Translated & edited by Thomas Cleary.

The Myth of Freedom, by Chögyam Trungpa.

Nine-Headed Dragon River, by Peter Matthiessen.

Returning to Silence: Zen Practice in Daily Life, by Dainin Katagiri. Foreword by Robert Thurman.

(*Continued on next page*)

Seeking the Heart of Wisdom: The Path of Insight Meditation, by Joseph Goldstein & Jack Kornfield. Foreword by H. H. the Dalai Lama.

Shambhala: The Sacred Path of the Warrior, by Chögyam Trungpa.

The Spiritual Teaching of Ramana Maharshi, by Ramana Maharshi. Foreword by C. G. Jung.

The Tantric Mysticism of Tibet, by John Blofeld.

Tao Teh Ching, by Lao Tzu. Translated by John C. H. Wu.

The Tibetan Book of the Dead: The Great Liberation through Hearing in the Bardo. Translated with commentary by Francesca Fremantle & Chögyam Trungpa.

The Way of the White Clouds: A Buddhist Pilgrim in Tibet, by Lama Anagarika Govinda. Foreword by Peter Matthiessen.

The Wheel of Life: The Autobiography of a Western Buddhist, by John Blofeld. Foreword by Huston Smith.

Zen Essence: The Science of Freedom. Translated & edited by Thomas Cleary.